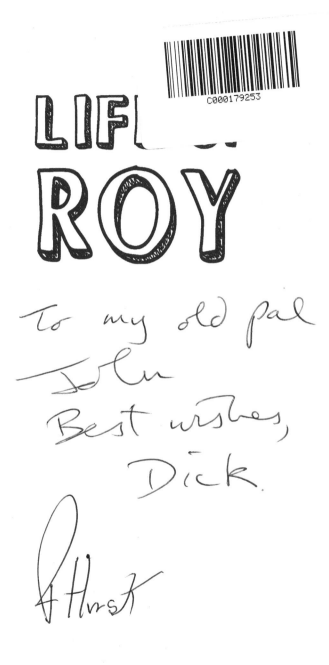

LIFE OF ROY

To my old pal
John
Best wishes,
Dick.

[signature]

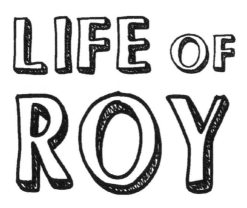

LIFE OF ROY

DOES HE TAKE SUGAR?

AS TOLD THROUGH CONVERSATIONS WITH
RICHARD DUNN

DAISA & CO

Life of Roy- Does He Take Sugar? published in Great Britain in 2019

Written by Richard Dunn and Roy Hirst

Copyright © Richard Dunn and Roy Hirst 2019

Photography © by Roy Hirst 2019

A CIP catalogue record for this book is available from the British Library.

Paperback ISBN 978-1-9162023-9-9

Book cover design by: Daisa & Co Publishing
Book Cover Image ©Shutterstock 1278692152, 158150951

Book typeset by:
DAISA & CO PUBLISHING
Barton upon Humber
North Lincolnshire
United Kingdom
DN18 5JR
www.daisapublishing.com

Printed in England

Daisa & Co Publishing is committed to a sustainable future for our business, our readers and our planet.
This book is made from paper certified by the Forestry Stewardship Council (FSC), an organisation dedicated to promoting responsible management of forest resources.

DEDICATION

Many things in our lives touch us in different ways. Through an accident, which resulted in my losing both legs, I have had to come to terms with being disabled. Hopefully, I have managed not only to learn to live with my disability but to also see the funny side of the difficulties it has created for my family and me.

This could only have been brought about with the love of my family; my wife Sheila, my four daughters, ten grandchildren and my mother Gladys and also the support of many good friends I have made over the years.

My thanks also go to the villagers of Ackworth who accepted my disability and me and this means more to me than they will ever know. Whoever reads my story, I do hope that one message comes through loud and clear.

Disability can be overcome with determination, a sense of humour and in my case, the support of a loving family and close friends.

Finally, my thanks to Dick Dunn, who has turned my thoughts and memories into this record of my life.

Roy Hirst

'And if I ever lose my legs then I won't moan and I won't beg.'

- 'Moon shadow' by Cat Stevens

CONTENTS

–

We are sitting on Roy's patio. The sun is baking hot and Roy is enjoying a quiet moment reflecting on his life.

The phone interrupts us four or five times while we talk. A Parish and County Councillor doesn't have much time for himself.

"Now where was I?" says Roy.

"Oh yes. I remember the whole thing as though it was yesterday..."

PROLOGUE

A heavy lorry is pounding along the narrow lane towards the village as boys and girls come running across the school playground on their way home for dinner.

"Fancy some fish and chips for your snap?" the bus driver asks his conductress.

"Good idea," she replies, "five minutes can't do much harm."

They park the bus next to the chip shop but also carelessly near the Belisha Crossing. The lorry thunders down the hill. The driver sees a clear road ahead except for an empty bus.

A little boy walking alone wonders where his friends are as they usually cross the road together but he's not worried. He feels safe and confident because he knows he must always cross the road at the Belisha Crossing.

In just a few seconds his life will change forever. Suddenly the lorry driver sees the six-year-old boy on the crossing but it is too late. Fate must take its course!

CHAPTER 1

THE EARLY YEARS

The pain was unbearable, but I never blacked out at any point. My legs were trapped between the wheel and the wheel arch, one severed completely, the other badly mangled. The wheel spun me round and I remember my head bouncing three or four times off the tarmac as I was tossed around like a rag doll.

They carried me to the verge and fortunately because we were outside the doctor's surgery I had help immediately. The tourniquet that the doctor applied to my leg probably saved my life and then I was rushed off to hospital.

I arrived there in agony, utterly bewildered and the first thing that happened was a male nurse slapped me really hard across the face. As a six-year-old, I didn't understand what I'd done to deserve that slap, but I knew I was going to tell my mum and dad when they arrived. It was only later in life I realised that his slap pulled me out of the severe shock I was sliding into.

At first, I was having two operations a week along with blood transfusions and I had to wait each time for them to come and put a mask over my face for the anaesthetic. I just hated that. Even today I can't stand anything over my face.

The treatment went on for years. I had skin grafts at Jimmy's in Leeds and operations to save my leg at the Infirmary in Pontefract. I lost my tibia in my lower leg and the muscles at the front of my shin were withered and torn. Useless really.

From six to twelve I was in and out of hospital regularly. My first stay was for a year. Time and time again I made friends with other boys who found themselves in the men's ward but they always went home and I didn't. I thought I would never go home. After that, I was in and out of hospital and stays of three to six months at a time weren't unusual.

Throughout this time I was in a men's ward with some very poorly people. Men came and went and many befriended me. I remember the rugby players who came in with broken noses and arms. I suppose I was spoilt rotten at times.

A hospital is a pretty boring place for a boy. My parents could only visit for two hours on an evening and so I had to find things to occupy myself. I suppose I was a little bugger when I put my mind to it. I remember crawling out of bed one night and yanking the tension ropes of a man who was strung up in traction. I'd never heard language like it!

Between operations I was at home and despite my injuries, like any boy I wanted to be out enjoying life. It was hard for my mum because I wasn't the sort you could wrap in cotton wool. When I was about ten years old, my leg began to bow.

I had no tibia and the constant strain of using the leg was making it buckle. The doctor said I would have to have my fibula broken and re-set, so back into hospital I went.

For six months my leg was in traction with a pin through my foot and all the way up to my knee so that it was completely immobilised. It was a lovely August day when I came out of hospital. I couldn't move much but I was itching to get out of the house so a few of my friends took me in a wheelchair. We took a bottle of water with bread and jam sandwiches and set off towards Wentbridge, which of course is miles away from Ackworth.

We only managed to get about half way there because it was steaming hot and it was hard work pushing me. We decided to turn round and make our way back along the banks of the River Went. Not the best idea we ever had. The pathway was overgrown and there were lots of styles to negotiate. Every time I reached a style I had to lever myself up, slide my bottom onto the style then swing my legs over, while my mates lifted my 'pram' over. This went on for at least an hour until we reached 'Slippy Bridge', a well-known beauty spot.

We sat on the bank watching the fish and generally messing around until I suggested that what we really needed was a swimming pool. The following day we met very early and set off armed with spades and sacking. Everything was loaded onto my wheelchair and off we went to create our swimming pool.

The River Went was only about six inches deep in August so we had a mammoth task on our hands. I sat on the bank of the river with a plastic sheet over my leg while we all attempted to turn the narrow fast flowing river into a square shaped pool. We filled the sacks with dirt and tied them together on the bottom of the riverbed but that wasn't enough to dam the water.

Fortunately we discovered some breeze blocks in the adjacent field that the farmer had been using to build a barn. It wasn't long before we had the perfect combination of bags and blocks to dam the water to a depth of about four feet. This piece of brilliant engineering had taken us ten hours to construct and by six o'clock that evening there was a number of parents looking for us. We missed both our dinner and tea.

The following morning we again set off early, expecting the water to have cleared and anticipating a day's swimming. On the way we noticed that the river seemed to be flooding its banks and we couldn't understand that because there had been no rain. By the time we reached the farmyard we knew something was wrong because there were lots of people and tractors and all sorts of feverish activity.

"What's the matter?" I asked. "What's the matter? I'll tell you what's-the-matter. Some idiots have blocked the river and it's flooding all the fields."

It didn't take them long to destroy our dam and ruin our swimming pool and I suppose that should have been the end of it.

After careful consideration and with our vast understanding of engineering matters, we came to the conclusion that we would have to re-design our pool! Any sensible person would now expect an escalating tale of disaster but the second time round we created the perfect swimming pool that provided a great deal of pleasure for many of us throughout a long hot summer. Picnics, swimming and fishing kept us happy for many an hour. They didn't supply me with a leg for a while but that didn't stop me.

Even when my friends weren't around I would go out in my wheelchair to find trees to climb. No one could climb a tree as fast as me. I remember one day the lowest branch of one particular tree was just too high to reach so I stood on my chair in order to get started.

As I jumped up to catch the branch I pushed the wheelchair over. Later, sitting happily in the bough of the tree I noticed the Turton's bus pull up. No one could see me in the tree but I could hear the conversations as people piled off the bus. I suppose I was quite famous by then and everyone recognised my wheelchair.

"He must have tipped out of his chair into the nettles or over the wall poor lad," came a frantic cry. Well my would-be rescuers searched for me in vain, but no one looked up until I let them in on my secret.

"Phone for the fire service," someone shouted.

"Look I'm all right, just leave me alone," I said.

Finally, they replaced my chair and I demonstrated how easy it was for me to climb out of a tree.

At the end of the holiday my friends went back to school but I was due in hospital for yet more treatment. I spent a few months in Castleford Hospital having my plaster cast removed and my leg straightened and then was allowed home for Christmas.

After the holidays it was back into hospital, Jimmy's this time for skin grafts. Mr Mortimer Shaw was the specialist and he decided to undertake a Pedicle Graft since I had very little skin on my leg. The procedure required cutting the skin on my stomach and rolling it up like a sausage but leaving it attached at one end so it would continue to grow.

My mum and dad borrowed a car to take me to hospital but because I was now in Leeds and they had very little money, I didn't see a lot of them. It was pretty boring for a young boy because my leg was attached to my stomach by the grafts and all I could do was lie in bed until they removed the skin and spread it across my legs.

I was wrapped in bandages for a month until eventually I was allowed to go home and believe me, that was such a relief. Like getting out of prison. (Not that I've ever been in prison!)

After only a couple of days I was back in St James' Hospital for another operation before coming home again for a few more days. The rest of the year was much the same.

I was in and out of hospital and before I had time to think, Christmas was round again.

By that time I had lost contact with most of my friends and because I was still having dressings on my leg, I couldn't go to school.

It was a pretty lonely time but I needed to escape from the house every day after being so confined all year. I loved nothing better than getting out in the fresh air and enjoying the countryside. I could sit for hours on the riverbank watching the animal life. One of my favourite pastimes was to wheel my chair into the river under 'Slippy Bridge' where I could sit watching the water shrews building nests.

I was interested in wildlife and learnt a lot at that time about nature. I watched rats and moles, birds and fish. Growing up in a village was a fantastic experience for a little boy. When the summer holidays finally arrived it was great meeting up with all my friends again and for a while, I could forget all about hospitals and operations.

My mum and dad had a lot to put up with. One time, with my friends, I dug a load of tunnels in our garden. For a while it kept me busy but they put a stop to it when one of my tunnels collapsed and our neighbour's hen hut disappeared underground.

For six months before I returned to school I had a tutor. Johnny Swinbank was a retired headmaster with a tendency to doze off when comfortable. My mum worked at the local chip shop during the day so it was just Mr Swinbank and me. He was a good old stick and I have fond memories of him. I suppose he was a bit of an eccentric but he was kind to me.

I always made sure that I had a glowing fire ready and it never took long before he would nod off. That was my chance to get out for an hour with my friends.

I was ten years old when I finally went back to school and I was way behind everyone else and to begin with, I couldn't understand what was happening. The first morning someone blew a whistle and all the other kids lined up. I just stood there until some guy manhandled me into one of the lines. We all marched into a big hall and were told to sit on the floor and shut up.

This was my first assembly but no one ever explained anything to me. It was all a bit daunting and I must have spent most of the first year learning the ropes. It's a lot different in schools today.

I was never keen on school but even when I tried to attend, things could go wrong. I remember this particular day. We were waiting at the water trough for Turton's bus to take us to school and as usual it was a double decker. Everyone piled upstairs and I thought, 'I'm not being left down here with all the old ones.' So I started to climb the stairs only to have my artificial leg break. A bolt snapped and proceeded to slide down my trouser leg, roll down the stairs, bounce off the platform and out of the door. Well there was such a commotion.

The driver pulled up so the conductor could go back to retrieve my bolt and quite a crowd gathered to see the bus turn around so they could take me home. You wouldn't see bus drivers doing that these days.

One of my favourite schoolteachers was Jim Keenan. When it was time for football, he would give Bill Storey and me the chance to tidy up his allotment, which was just across the road from the school. We really loved that, particularly as Jim, a heavy smoker, would give us a couple of cigs to do the job. We would sit in his shed thinking we were the bee's knees.

It got to the point where I absolutely hated school. I couldn't understand or tolerate the rules and because of spending so much time at home or in hospital, I had become a 'free spirit' or maybe I was spoilt!

I wasn't the only one who didn't like school. A few of us had a regular routine where we would register in the morning then disappear over the school wall on our way to the toilet. No one seemed too bothered and we spent the day happily occupying ourselves. Some days would be spent at Bill Storey's house making tea and playing records. Other days we would be on the mud heaps looking for coal to sell down the street.

About this time I learnt about the joys of farming. We would bunk off school to 'tattee pick' and 'pea pull'. It was hard graft and sometimes I went home soaked to the skin but the money was good and anything was better than school. Despite my artificial leg I never felt different from anyone else and I wanted to live life to the full.

I was a strong and active lad and both ready and able to take on any task or challenge. At that time I struck up a close friendship with the farmhands who taught me to drive the tractor.

There was only one foot pedal so I became adept at manoeuvring the tractor and could hitch up the trailer as well as anyone. In the summer I would help with the harvesting and that was when I began to pile on the muscle. You know, lifting and pitchforking bales of hay. I may have had an unconventional education, but I did learn a lot about life that stood me in good stead later.

I suppose that losing my leg as I did had a pretty profound effect on my character and outlook. I'd lived much of my youth in an adult environment and I'd learnt to think for myself. There were people who thought that I should accept my disability and be content to sit in my wheelchair. Not me. I couldn't see how I was different and I was determined to live life to the full.

Roy and his brother, Steve

Roy on his uncle's boat

CHAPTER 2

WILD YOUTH

I had what you might describe as a 'wild youth'. I was impetuous and headstrong and always one for having a laugh. At first, I would hang about the village with my mates, usually on the seat at Moortop but as we reached our late teens we went further afield, on our motorbikes.

There were about thirty of us and we would drive in convoy to York, Tadcaster and on one occasion, Gretna Green. When we weren't travelling, we spent our time in local pubs and dance halls wearing designer suits, (mine was black with a red velvet collar and cuffs) and listening to juke boxes. I have fond memories of driving to Bridlington and having bonfires on the beach. I've always been interested in vehicles and when one or two of my friends bought motorbikes I felt I needed to keep up. I couldn't afford the sort of motor bike the others were getting so I bought an old '350 Arial Square Four' motorbike from a lad in Featherstone.

It wasn't roadworthy and I had to keep it in my pigeon hut (yes, I raced pigeons at the time).

I stripped it down and eventually got it going. I put a 'straight-through-mega' into the exhaust system to by-pass the mufflers in the silencer. I might have had the slowest bike in the group but it sounded the part. I lowered the seat to accommodate my leg and added cow-horn handlebars. With my long hair flowing in the breeze (no crash helmets in those days) I looked like an extra from the film `Easy Rider'.

The first day I had it running I fired it up and rode up and down our street on it. The old bloke from Number 3 came out and flagged me down.

"Hey up, old cock," he shouted, "Have you got any string?"

"No, why?" I asked, looking a bit puzzled.

"To tie me telly down," was his simple reply. I got the message.

I was eligible for a three-wheeler invalid carriage, which had a small Villiers engine and to try to keep up with the lads I needed to make some improvements because by the time I arrived at our destination, everyone else was on their way home.

I knew a mechanic from Harding's and I asked him if he could get a bigger 650 Villiers water cooled engine in exchange for a ton of coal. A deal was struck. I decided to customise it so I cut out the roof of this Government Property carriage and did a paint job on the light sky blue paint. I sprayed it a camouflage design and fitted a convertible roof from an old sports car. It might not have kept the rain out but everyone thought it looked pretty good.

All the bikers would congregate at the seat on the top of the hill. It wasn't long before we were competing against each other. The challenge was to see who could race down the hill and round the bend at Carr Bridge the fastest. It became a craze and bikers came from all over to have a go. I had to carry a bag of sand on the front wheel to compensate for the power of the engine; otherwise I'd have gone into orbit!

With my 'souped up' invalid carriage I was unbeatable. I would take the bend on two wheels (some still swear blind it was one wheel). Rich Hook had the fastest bike but I think I still hold the record for that little run. My vehicle was something of a talking point with all the bikers and everyone would gather round wherever I went. On one occasion I decided to go to Doncaster to give it a good run and although it was only built for one I took my mate Harvey with me.

Heading back home the road was reasonably quiet so I let the throttle out. I don't know how fast I was going because the speedometer's maximum speed only went up to 60 mph. We were going so fast that the top of the car kept blowing off and we had to put it in the back.

Between Doncaster and Upton a black Zephyr with a blue light on top pulled out in front of me. I was motoring at such a speed that there was no way I could stop so I overtook the police car and disappeared like a bat out of hell. When we arrived in Ackworth we pulled up outside the chip shop and started laughing our heads off.

I was laughing so much I didn't notice the dark car slowly pulling up alongside us.

Well, I ended up in court on a charge of reckless driving and was given a £3 fine. The trial was not without its funny moments though. The arresting officer, reading from his notes, began his statement, "I was overtaken by an invalid carriage travelling at an approximate speed of 80 to 90 miles per hour."

At that point the magistrate stopped him and asked, "Would you read that out again?"

I thought at that point I might get acquitted because no one in his or her right mind could imagine an invalid carriage going that speed. Three days after the trial, a man from the Ministry came and confiscated my machine and it was six months before I could persuade them to let me have it back.

When I was about eighteen years old, summer or winter, whatever the weather, I still met my friends at the old wooden seat outside the doctors' surgery on Moortop Hill and at that time there was one girl in particular that took a shine to me. I suppose she was about 16 years old and she'd been pestering me to take her for a ride in my invalid carriage. I was a bit reluctant because I wasn't supposed to carry passengers. To be honest, I'd been caught doing that a few times and I didn't want to get her in trouble. Also in the back of my mind, I thought her parents didn't think much of me anyway. In the end she talked me into it and we went for a drive to Low Ackworth and I parked up near Bernard Slacher's farm, about twenty feet from the road.

I switched off the engine and lights and we made ourselves comfortable. She had to be home by 8 pm so we only had about half an hour. We sat in the dark talking and it was really pleasant and cosy. It wasn't long before the car began to overheat. It was like being in a sauna. We both said at once, "My god, it's getting hot in here."

Trust me, it wasn't anything of a romantic nature I was doing that was sending the thermometer off the scale. I tried to open the window for some fresh air and there was such a smell. I shut it quickly because air wasn't the only thing coming in through that window!

I thought, 'Better get out of here and quick,' but the car engine only spluttered. I tried to put the headlights on so I could see what was happening but to no avail. It was at this point I got that terrible sinking feeling. I mean the car was actually sinking. I couldn't open the door because the windows were now at ground level. My girl started to panic.

I can't blame her because we were trapped and the cab was now steaming hot. Me being me of course, was being my usual relaxed self.

"It's okay love we'll be alright," I said, in a voice one octave higher than usual. After another ten minutes even I'm beginning to panic. I'm working out the odds between being buried alive or roasted to death.

At 7.45pm, she began to cry. "We're never going to get out of here."

It took me all my time to keep her calm and I was telling her, "If the worst comes to the worst, I'll smash my way out."

I didn't believe my own reassurances though because the car had a metal roof and sides. Even I wasn't that strong. Just after 8 pm when even I'd given up all hope, I saw a light in the distance. As the light approached I started shouting at the top of my voice. The light was from a bloke on a bike and at first he couldn't see us.

"Over here, over here," I shouted and finally he spotted us. Luckily he was one of the farm hands who had been working late. He said, "This looks a right mess. I can't help you on my own. I'll have to get my boss and a tractor."

It didn't take him long to return with the tractor and they hooked the car onto it to set about pulling us out. The first attempt wasn't too successful because all they did was pull the top off my three-wheeler. Could have taken my head off! The smell was terrible and at last we realised what the problem was. The farmer had dug a pit and filled it with hen muck in order that later in the season, he could spread it on the fields. Of course, the pit had developed a hard crust and I'd parked inadvertently on top of a pile of excrement.

While I'd been romancing this young girl, my trusty vehicle had been sinking slowly into the mire. The smell was awful but so was the heat and once they'd pulled the top off my car we were covered in this festering brew.

The farmer kindly took my girl home and I waited in the car for a tow. They eventually got me out and I'm not sure which was in the worse condition, the three-wheeler or me.

The next day I rang the garage. "It's Roy Hirst here," was all I needed to say.

"We'll send the pick-up truck," was the short reply. They knew what I was like.

"Don't bother with the pick-up truck, just bring a wheelbarrow," I replied.

Eventually I moved to a more respectable mode of transport. I hadn't passed my test when I bought my first car. It was a Ford Zephyr 4, ivory white and brand spanking new. Dad went with me to collect it because I hadn't passed my test. Geoff Garbett, a mate of mine, sat in with me until I passed my test. In those days there were servo-assisted air tanks in the boot of your car and I had it about four days when I pulled up on the top of Moor Top Hill to see my old mates.

Instead of starting the engine I just cruised down the hill to where they were all sitting and pulled across the road to park outside the church. My mates saw me and came running across the road. I hit my brakes and nothing happened. Somehow I'd pumped all the air out of the servo-assisted system. I shouldn't have worried about stopping because there was a wall, telegraph pole and street bench readily available to counteract the force of gravity. I came to a shuddering stop. When I reversed the car and jumped out for a look I couldn't believe it, both wings were as flat as a pancake and my lovely new car seemed ruined. I had a right lump in my throat.

When I was seventeen, the lads decided that we were going to have a week at Butlin's Holiday Camp. Nine of us went and you've never seen a crew like it in your life.

First thing we did was to have a look round. Among the shops there was one selling shoes and I saw the best pair of winkle pickers I've ever seen in my life. They were white and sharp as a needle; 'They're mine, they are.' I thought.

That night I went out dancing in my bottle green suit with drainpipe trousers and of course, my new white winkle pickers. I tell you what; it was the business. I wasn't much good at dancing but that night I was on the dance floor: bit of dancing, bit of bopping, bit of chatting up and snogging.

I went back to this girl's chalet and we were sat on her bed in the dark. I had my arm round her and she felt my leg and says, "What's this?"

"It's my artificial leg, love."

"Well it's cold," she replies. So I say, "Don't worry, I'm going to take it off in a minute."

So I took my leg off and put it to one side and she started arguing with me and accusing me of taking her for granted and just after 'one thing'.

I said, "No, no love, I was just trying to get more comfortable." She wouldn't believe me of course and I can't blame her. Before I could move she jumped up and ran out of the room taking my leg with her and half of a pair of my white winkle pickers.

I shouted for my mate. "Mel, she's taken my bloody leg." So Mel jumped up and with a few other lads goes after her. They found her by the boating lake but there was no sign of my leg. You can imagine; I was hopping mad. She wouldn't come back to the chalet or tell them what she'd done with my leg so they organised a search party while I sat stranded.

I was quite upset because although I didn't mind if my leg ended up in the boating lake, my winkle picker was another matter altogether! They retraced her steps and after a considerable search, ended up finding it in one of the boats. Two days later we met again and made up and we were together after that for about twelve months.

We certainly got out and about in those days. I remember thirty of us going to Blackpool on the bus. First thing you do is sink a few drinks then into the fun fair. Well, it was brilliant for a young lad but what impressed me most was `Blackpool Tower'. Oh, what a building. I was about nineteen years old and I'd had a few drinks so I was up for a challenge. We went up the lift and then up the steps right onto the top platform. I could see a work deck above us but there was a 'No Entry' sign on the access gate. An enormous lock and chain were hanging on the gate but the workmen painting the structure above us had left the gate open.

A few of us decided to ignore the sign and climb up. I took the last few steps through a hatch which led outside and clambered up to within four feet of the flagpole right on the top of the tower. I was afraid of nothing at that age and took a dare to climb down the outside of the building to the first floor on the Inspection ladder. So I thought, 'I'm on for this.' I was strong and could hold on to anything. I did it without any problems and there were thirty guys waiting for me. I expected a round of applause but instead I got the police. They'd had to clear everyone away from the base of the tower in case I fell and they were not at all pleased at the antics of this daft teenager.

They didn't arrest me, just gave me the `Scarborough Warning' and told me how stupid I was. A few days later, looking back on it all, I knew that I'd been daft but strangely enough, ever since then I've wanted to do it again! I quite fancied mountain climbing after that.

During my wild youth I gained quite a reputation as a hard man. It began I suppose, when I was about fifteen years old. I was standing in Pontefract bus station with all my friends. There was about eight of us. We'd been to the pictures and some of the lads had gone to the lavatory. It was the first time I'd been out on the town. Suddenly one of my pals came running past with his nose bleeding and shouted, "Don't stand there, they're coming after us."

Well I couldn't resist. I had to go and have a look for myself. When I walked through the door I could see there was a big gang of lads knocking `seven bells' out of my friends. I'd no sooner walked in than this big fellow with enormous teeth (I'd never seen teeth like them!) set about me. I didn't get the chance to say a word before he hit me. He gave me a right 'going over'.

Three weeks later, I was back in Pontefract at the pictures. My parents had told me not to go because they didn't want me coming home battered and bruised, but I wasn't going to let that stop me. Sure enough, just as we came around the corner from the bus station this gang of lads was waiting for us. I thought, 'There's no way they're going to catch me out again.'

The guy with the big teeth was there and I could tell from his face he wasn't just going to say, 'Hello, how are you going on?'

'Get in first, Roy,' I told myself and as soon as he was within reach I decked him. The punch was a beauty. I hit him so hard I could feel the judder right up my arm. He hit the floor and didn't get up. Of course, pandemonium broke out as both gangs of lads pitched in.

That was the start of a new career for me. From then on I took no lip from anyone and I was scared of no one. I got my retaliation in first. The down side of this was that word spread and I had a reputation for being a hard man, a bit of a big hitter. No matter where I went after that lads were coming up and challenging me to a fight. I was a big lad and really fit, a keep fit fanatic with some experience in the Martial Arts. No one was going to push me around.

I suppose I've carried that philosophy through life. I've championed a few causes in my time and never been afraid to do what's right. One fight that comes to mind when I was about 15 years old, was when we were in the 'Welfare' in Ropergate and me and Trevor Hardacre were having a coke while eyeing the place up.

It was really packed. I was told not to go on the dance floor as some Pontefract lads were looking for me. I was standing by a wall, 30 – 40 of them all around me trying to throw punches at the same time. Being me, I dived on the biggest one and ended up on the floor. The next thing this big lad is standing on my chest trying to cave it in. I was thrown down the stairs and hit a car parked at the bottom.

I had a broken nose, five loose teeth, a split head and no sleeves left in my coat. I went to casualty to be stitched up and then home. I tried to sneak in but mum was waiting for me. She went berserk.

The next day I came downstairs not feeling in the best of health. I had two black eyes, a busted lip and aching teeth. At about 11am Trevor knocked on the door. I noticed he had a nasty graze on his knuckles. He told me to get my coat, as we were going out.

I said I wasn't up to it but he said, "I know where they are. They're hanging out at Willy Oates' Billiard Hall."

We climbed the stairs into this massive room. Trevor asked about a bloke called 'Ginner'.

He wasn't there so we went back down the stairs. Two of them followed us so we decked them and ran off. We headed down to the Baghill part of town where Ginner Bryant lived.

We knocked on his door and when he answered I dragged him out and we started scrapping in his garden. His dad came out to see what was going on so I explained to him that I was there to avenge the hammering his son had given me the night before.

"Nay lad," he replied, "Ginner was at home all last night with me and his mum."

I didn't know what to say. I knew straight away I was in the wrong but it's hard to apologise at that age. Trevor and I just slunk off. It worked out okay in the end.

Five weeks later the Pontefract and Ackworth gangs got together to sort out the Sherburn lads who were hanging around our patch. Ginner Bryant became a good friend and still is today.

When I was in my early twenties, I was engaged to a girl from Airedale. I was still very young and impetuous and one night I was drinking with some mates at the White Swan. We were having a private party; you know a 'lock in', when some lads tried to gate-crash. There was a bit of a to-do so I pitched in and helped chuck some of them out. Viv Nicholson was there. She was the woman who was famous for winning the pools and had caused a sensation in the papers with the headlines:

'I'm going to SPEND! SPEND! SPEND!'

She invited me back to her house and I ended up stopping for about 18 months. Needless to say my engagement was off. Viv's husband Keith had been killed in a car crash on his way home from the races and what with death duties and the lifestyle they had enjoyed, she no longer had money to throw around. Having said that, her house was the first I'd been in with plush fitted carpets, curtains and central heating. I always found Viv to be a kind, genuine person and all the talk of the wild parties was rubbish. I suppose the money went to her and Keith's head and for a while they lived the good life.

Roy with Derek Alderman

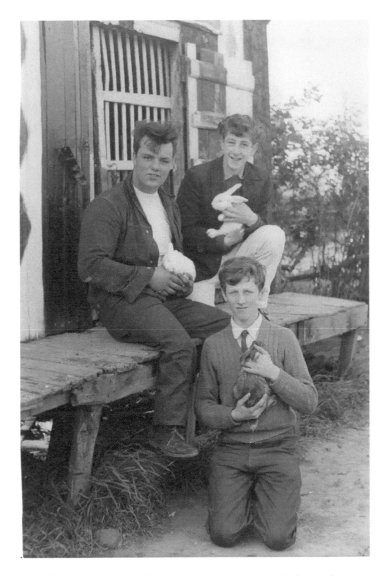

Roy with Keith Wood and Maurice Edwards

CHAPTER 3

WORKING WITH ONE LEG

I was fifteen years old when I started work. I was a boiler man at Bramley's Steam Laundry in Leeds. I got up at 5am every day and the bus brought me home at half past eight in the evening. I shovelled five ton of coal a day and removed clinker from the boiler. I was lucky I suppose because although I only had half a good leg, I was strong and could physically pull myself through.

The job only lasted six months. The laundry was in a smokeless zone and my boiler was old and no matter what I tried, it would sometimes billow smoke. There were complaints from the locals and the manager demanded that I sweep the chimney. To do this I would have had to climb thirty feet to the top of the boiler, crawl through a tiny metal door and then brush the walls of the ninety-foot chimney while scaling a metal ladder. What he was ordering me to do was so unfair and I just let rip.

I shoved a brush in one of his hands and a shovel in the other and before he could react I had him up the first few steps to the boiler. His feet never touched the floor.

"Do it yourself. I quit," I bawled. I said a few other things as well but they are unprintable.

I don't suppose he took my advice as to where to put the pressure gun. I never was paid for that last week's work. I was young, impetuous and had a lot to learn about life but I knew what was right and fair and this was a valuable experience for me. I suppose I've spent the rest of my life fighting injustice and sticking up for the ordinary man and woman in the street

I went to work with friends at Barnby Dun Power Station. I was 400ft. up, erecting scaffolding and laying shuttering; that's putting wooden shutters down so that concrete can be laid. I loved every minute of it. I was up there for six months and was earning great money but then they introduced new health and safety rules and I was grounded. They said I wasn't fit to be up there and I suppose they were right in a way. I could have had the tea boy's job, looking after the lads when they came back down. I couldn't do that, not after I'd been part of it all. So they set me on dumper driving and that was okay.

I then moved on to driving those big Earth Scrapers but I could only drive them on the land, not on the roads where most of the money was to be earned. Mind you, I put in a lot of overtime and I was earning £50 to £60 a week when average wages were only £15 to £20. I was fortunate.

I was never one to sit around on my backside doing nothing, even though I had a disability.

For a time I worked at Resell Processes in the mould shop where they made mouldings for packaging. There was no heating and we would have to break the ice off the machines each winter morning before we could begin work. My leg constantly troubled me. Sometimes I'd work for six months, sometimes just for six weeks and then it would break down and I'd be off work again.

During this period I also tried to earn a bit of extra cash by helping my brother Steve renovate old cars, which we then sold at auctions. We were complete novices when we started but somehow managed to make money without too many problems. I remember coming home from work and finding my brother Steve and his mate looking at an old Ford Anglia car in our back garden. The front end was a bit of a mess but Steve thought the engine and gearbox were good. I said, "Let me have a look at it after dinner. See if I can patch it up."

When I was ready to start, I found my brother trying to stick bits of filler onto the front wings to no avail. The faster he put it on the faster it fell off.

"That's no good," I said. "Let me have a look."

I decided in my naivety that what we needed was chicken wire. I moulded the wire into a rough shape and then fastened it onto the car. Next came the papier-mâché! I was creating the sort of masterpiece that these days would win the Turner Prize.

Once I had a base to work on, I started to 'lash on' the body filler. There were lumps and bumps everywhere but I just kept adding the filler.

After hours of smoothing off with 'wet and dry', the first wing looked pretty good and using the same technique I soon had the second wing finished. So this was the start of a new career. I bought some coach paint and a brush and by the time I'd finished it looked pretty good when the sun was at the correct angle. I painted two red stripes along the sides and one down the middle. It certainly looked the part. Unfortunately when we took it for a spin, we discovered that the main shaft drive was bent and every time the car went over thirty miles per hour it began to violently shudder.

What we needed now was a couple of better tyres and someone even dafter than us to sell the car on. We decided to try the local scrap yard in our search for cheap tyres and the scrap dealer Mr Lloyd let us scour his yard.

"Nice car, you have there lads," he said with obvious interest. "Did you know I bought and sold cars?"

Well we did but we weren't going to admit it.

Play daft and see what happens,' I thought.

We asked him if he would like a drive and we took him around the yard at a very sedate speed and never more than thirty miles per hour.

"I'll give you sixty quid for it," he offered.

"No thanks," I said as coolly as I could.

"We'll get one hundred and fifty for this little beauty at the auctions."

"One hundred and I'm robbing myself," he protested. He thought he was pulling a fast one but I knew better.

"It's a deal," I managed to say with a straight face, although I wanted to snatch the money and run for it. Three weeks later we were back at the scrap yard and we had a very frosty reception from Mr Lloyd. I'd have made a good poker player because I stood with a concerned expression on my face as he explained how he had had a buyer who took the Anglia for a test drive.

"The car started to shudder violently and then the wings fell off," Mr Lloyd complained.

"That's terrible," I sympathized. "Do you want me to try and fix it?"

"No fear," or words to that effect, was his reply.

Eventually, I became very professional at fixing up cars but couldn't always find the time. One day I had four cars lined up and no time to work on them, so I thought I'd 'throw a sicky'.

I went to see Doctor McRoberts and fed him a line about a bad back. He was a lovely man and we started nattering. Of course, I left without my sick note. Two hours later, with the paint compressor droning away, I could just about hear a knock on the garage door. Opening the door at that point would have meant the dust and rubbish blowing in and my masterpiece being ruined.

"Bugger off, I'm busy," I shouted over the noise.

I thought whoever it was had left, but two minutes later there was an even louder knock, so reluctantly I covered up the car and opened the door.

The phrase, 'What the hell do you want,' was just forming on my lips when I saw who it was and the words that actually came out were, "Hello Doctor." Doctor McRoberts was standing there with my sick note. I was caught red handed in work clothes and mask!

"I don't think you'll be needing this, Mr Hirst," was all he said.

That was another thing I didn't get away with.

CHAPTER 4

SETTLING DOWN

I was in Jimmy's in Leeds having skin grafts when I met Sheila. She was a trainee nurse assigned to the plastic surgery ward and had to write a case study on me.

At this point a voice from the kitchen interrupted, "Mum got the short straw then!"

"No one asked for your opinion, Mel," Roy retorted.

I'd been laid on my back for six months with a bolt through my foot so they could apply traction to my leg, which had a cage over it for protection. From knee to toe they had removed my skin and most of my muscle and they wanted to try a new kind of graft. They took skin from my chest and arms to graft layer after layer onto my shin.

I was 21 years old, covered in bandages and had one leg strung up when I met the love of my life.

I had all my own hair and teeth then but didn't feel much else belonged to me.

Sheila asked me to describe my accident and I spun her a yarn about working for Billy Smarts' Circus and an elephant taking a dislike to me. She spent half an hour taking notes and wasn't too pleased when I finally confessed I was having her on.

Not the best start to a relationship but we became friends quickly after that. We just hit it off. They took the pin out of my foot and I was allowed to sit up. I was as dizzy as a cuckoo. Sheila asked me if I was okay, but I had this terrible pain in my back and I couldn't stop drinking. During the night I started being sick and then, as my condition grew more serious, I passed in and out of consciousness. They rushed me to the Renal Unit at Leeds General Hospital because it looked as though my kidneys had shut down.

They sent for my mum and dad because they thought I was a 'goner' but believe me, I had no intentions of going anywhere. I don't suppose I was playing with a full pack at that stage but I swear I heard the swish of the curtains and the biggest man I've ever seen in my life appeared. He must have been 7'9". He wore a white gown, a large hat and wellies and carried a scalpel. He had those thick horned rimmed glasses and to tell you the truth, he scared the life out of me. He said something about cutting my vein and inserting a shunt. I hadn't got a clue what he was talking about but if I was scared at the sight of him, I was petrified about what he was threatening to do.

"We're going to hook you up for dialysis," he said, pointing at this massive machine in the corner of the room. I suppose technology has moved on over the years but this thing looked like a combined harvester.

I think it was terror that came to my rescue and cured me. I wasn't allowed to drink because my body was flooding with fluid but I just couldn't stop myself. Bandaged from top to bottom I still managed to pull myself onto the sink unit and I drank and drank and drank from out of the tap.

I was shaking and traumatised and had not peed for three days but then the floodgates opened so to speak. The nurses couldn't keep up with me. I filled three bottles, two bedpans and then wet the bed.

Lying on my back for six months had meant that a lot of sediment had gathered in my kidneys and when I sat up, the sediment had blocked my tubes. They cleared in the end and eventually I got back to normal. That night though I felt lonely and lost and then this beautiful face appeared. It was Sheila.

She wasn't wearing her uniform and she looked a real treat. I was so pleased she had come to visit me. We talked for two hours non-stop and I forgot all about my bits of aches and pains. She visited me the night after for three hours and I suppose we've never really been apart since.

When I returned to Jimmy's from the Renal Unit, I was feeling a lot better and some of my friends in the ward decided to throw me a welcome back party in the day room. We had beer and sandwiches smuggled in and I decided to play a prank on one of the ward sisters. She was one of the 'old school'. You know the type: a real battle-axe. If she had caught us celebrating we'd have all been for the high jump.

I took my leg and dressed it in trousers and a shoe and then hung it out of the window, you know those old sash windows and then pulled it down trapping the bottom of the leg. It looked pretty convincing. It looked as though we'd hung someone out the window! The idea was that we'd just sit quietly and wait for her to arrive but we were in hysterics. We couldn't stop laughing and one poor man burst all the stitches in his mouth. He'd had a wisdom tooth removed and suddenly blood came spurting out of his mouth like a fountain. There was blood everywhere. I think he'd been having a good time until then but I never did find out because I was banned from going anywhere near him after that.

We had to buzz for help and the first person to appear was the 'sergeant major.' I think I misjudged her. I thought she would be calm and collected. You know, the ultimate professional. I thought she could cope with the sight of all the blood. It was the man hanging from the window that tipped her over the edge. She just started screaming until help arrived. The blood soaked man was rushed off to theatre and I got a right rollicking. My legs, arms and chest became infected so I was quite ill again but during that time Sheila and I became very close. When I finally left hospital Sheila came with me. She lived with my mum and dad until we were married.

The day after I came out of hospital I went to pick Sheila up at the end of her shift but on the way home we were involved in an accident. A policeman arrived and asked me to get out of the car and when I said I couldn't he opened the driver's door.

"Oh my God, lad," was all he could gasp when he saw me. I don't think he could quite believe what he was looking at. It looked as though I'd dressed for the accident. I was still bandaged from head to toe and had a pot on one leg. Did you ever see the film, 'The Return of the One-Legged Mummy'?

That was the start of our courtship. We were engaged after nine months and married in a year. My leg was so bad that I couldn't wear shoes so I did most of my courting in wellies. I've always been a bit of a romantic but no one could have called me debonair at that time.

When we were going somewhere special, I would have my trousers out but most of the time they were just tucked into the top of my wellies. Sheila must have loved me to put up with all that.

We were married in 1967 at a small chapel in Woodborough, Nottinghamshire, which was Sheila's home. The chapel was packed and afterwards we had a sit down meal in the village hall. I had a new pair of shoes by then and when I knelt down in the chapel, I'd left the price tag on the soles for everyone to see.

I had a white Zephyr 4 at that time and when we left the reception we found our friends had gone to town decorating it. Tin cans, balloons and all sorts of messages written in pink and blue toothpaste.

What a sight. We set off to cheers and waves on our way to the Eden Hotel in London but within four miles I had to stop to change a punctured tyre. That was just our first stop. We had to stop four more times to ask directions. I was a country boy and I hadn't a clue where I was going. The first time we stopped a very helpful policeman gave us directions. Sheila and I both noticed his smart blue trousers were covered in pink toothpaste.

"Thanks very much," I said, and before it could dawn on him what had happened, I sped off like Michael Schumacher.

We didn't reach the hotel until midnight and on the twelfth chime of the hotel clock, without a word of a lie, all four tyres on the car went flat. It's a good job I'm not superstitious! At that moment a young porter appeared.

"Any luggage to be carried in, Sir?" He asked.

"Yes, but you can start with me," was my reply.

It was so late we just snuggled down for the night and looked forward to starting married life fully the following morning. No such luck. At some ungodly hour there was a knock on our door and when I answered it, a young lass was standing there in her nightdress.

"Have you got a key to Room 25? I've locked myself out," she sobbed.

I could see she was frantic but there wasn't anything I could do, I had my bride waiting for me.

"Sorry dear, but I'm on my honeymoon," I said with what I thought was a knowing nod of the head.

She didn't understand and it took ages before the penny dropped. "Oh!" she exclaimed at last. At that point she turned and retreated down the corridor looking decidedly embarrassed. Of course by now it was time for breakfast and we had to hurry down to the dining room. I felt a bit out of my depth at breakfast. It was the first time I'd stayed in a hotel and I didn't know the protocol. They brought me half a grapefruit in a glass dish and I had to ask Sheila which spoon to use. By the end of breakfast I thought I'd carried everything off very well for a novice, until I realised that I was still wearing my pyjama top!

After our wedding Sheila and I moved into a house in Bell Lane. We didn't have much. We had a massive kitchen and we covered the floor with blue and white 'Marley Tiles' since they were the fashion in those days. We had to take turns sitting down in the kitchen because although we had a fridge and a cooker we could only afford one chair. Like most newly-weds in those days, we had very little but it was fantastic to be in our own house. Both sets of parents were really helpful, giving us bits and pieces but even with all the help, we couldn't afford carpets and in the front room there was only a three-piece suite and a rug.

CHAPTER 5

FIVE FEET SIX TO
SIX FEET FOUR

I was working at Jackson's Glass Works when I finally had my second leg amputated. I was a married man with a little one. Rachel had been born in 1968 and I needed to work, so every day for a year, I negotiated the fire escape at Jackson's to earn a living. One winter day when the fire escape was icy, I slipped and broke my kneecap. I had to go on compensation, compo, they called it then, and again I was back at home.

My leg had been giving me some serious problems for some time. I was living with constant pain and kept developing infections. The doctor felt that the deterioration in the condition of my leg was becoming life threatening and that I might even have cancer.

I didn't have cancer as it turns out, but to be on the safe side, the doctor had removed most of my leg leaving me with yet another three-inch stump. Apparently my heart had stopped during the operation and the surgeon had to shock me to get it going again. Good job these people knew what they were doing!

I woke up surrounded by sandbags, which had been strategically placed to stop me from moving while my stump healed. Fortunately for me I was a very fast healer and in only two days they were able to remove the drip that was attached to my leg. In three more days I was allowed home but not before I'd made a fool of myself in front of my GP. I'd punched a hole in the bottom of a paper bottle used for peeing in, meaning to play a prank on a miserable old man in my ward but someone switched the bottles and I ended up getting a right soaking just as Mr McWilliams arrived to see me. I'll never change. Anything for a laugh!

Two days after I was discharged from the hospital there was a knock on the door and a doctor I hadn't seen before swept into our living room. I thought at first it was a local GP come to see how I was but this guy had come to see me about my compo claim.

"I need to have a look at your knee-cap Mr Hirst," he says, smiling at me.

"Well that could be a problem Doctor," I smile back at him, "because I don't know what the hospital has done with it. It's probably been incinerated by now."

I've never seen a man's face change colour so fast.

I think he was more worried about the compensation than what had happened to my leg. He turned white as a sheet.

"Do you mind if I sit down Mr Hirst?"

"Not at all Doctor. Would you like a cup of tea?"

Over a nice cup of tea, I explained that my missing kneecap could not be laid at Jackson's door but was the result of long-term illness.

He went away a more sober man than he arrived and needless to say we never saw him again. Walking with artificial legs was always going to be a problem from now on.

I have a long body but my leg was so badly damaged that I was only 5'6" before my operation. My new artificial legs were designed in proportion with my body so suddenly I'm 6'4".

Ten weeks after my operation I began to learn how to walk again. It was probably the hardest thing I had ever done. I was supposed to pull myself out of a chair placed between two parallel bars and learn to stand for a few minutes. My stumps were still very raw and I expect the doctors knew best, but I was in a rush to get on with my life. Whenever the nurse left I would think, 'bugger this' and start walking up and down.

I was determined to walk in record time and of course it wasn't long before the skin on my stumps began to break down. I was told that bath salts and methylated spirits would harden the skin so I started myself on a regime of salt baths and spirit rub. I wish someone had told me not to use undiluted 'meth's' because the pain was excruciating but it did the job.

It didn't take me long to master walking with my new legs but I can't describe the sweat and pain I had to go through. As soon as I was able to get around again the Department of Health and Social Security called me for an examination by one of its doctors. His office turned out to be up a flight of stairs and there was no lift available.

Sheila went upstairs to explain the situation to the doctor. If I'd expected any sympathy I didn't get any. The doctor, brisk and uncompromising explained, "Douglas Bader fought a war with two false legs and there are plenty of people with worse conditions than you Mr Hirst. If you put your mind to it, you can get up these stairs. Come on, I'll help you."

I couldn't refuse an invitation like that.

"Okay Doctor," I said, feeling a bit guilty. "I'll give it a go." I had more chance of playing centre forward for England than getting up those stairs and on the second step I almost fell backwards onto the good doctor who by now was covered in sweat and beginning to question the sanity of this particular exercise.

"Bend your other leg, man," came the exasperated cry.

"I can't. It's made of wood," I said with just a hint of irritation. At that point, on the edge of calamity and with nerves fraying, the penny finally dropped.

"You've got two false legs Mr Hirst?"

"It's all in my notes doctor. Are we going up or down?"

Douglas Bader had his legs removed from his knees and all credit to the man, he could fly a plane. I was balanced precariously on a flight of stairs with only three-inch stumps and an instinct for survival keeping me upright. Once I was back on ground level the doctor apologised and said he would make sure I wasn't asked to attend this clinic again.

Six months later a letter arrived with an appointment with the same doctor in the same room. This time I knew exactly what to do and not surprisingly, Sheila refused to come into the building with me. When I reached the bottom of those stairs I levered myself down and lay prostrate on the floor.

"Help, help!" I shouted at the top of my voice. "I've fallen down the stairs."

The doctor and nurse arrived at the top of the stairs together and looked down in horror at me spread-eagled on the floor. Time seemed to stand still. They seemed to be struck dumb and rooted to the spot like a couple of statues.

I thought I'd better say something.

"Roy Hirst, Doctor, I've come for my ten o'clock appointment." What a palaver. Everyone started rushing around in a panic. The doctor and nurse were really nice to me and very helpful but they never invited me for another appointment.

The year Rachel was born, the government introduced a mobility scheme and I knew a few people more able bodied than me who had applied and got it.

I had a little three-wheeler, 'invalid carriage' they called them, to help me get around but this would be the chance for me to have a car. I would be able to take my family out and have a bit more of a normal life. I filled in the forms and was asked to attend an interview at Hemsworth.

"How far can you walk Mr Hirst?"

Well, you want to be optimistic in situations like this.

Most disabled people in my experience don't want others to know how difficult it is to do those ordinary things that everyone else takes for granted. I suppose it's about pride and self-respect.

"About fifty yards on a good day," was my honest but naïve reply. I didn't mention the pain I would be in or the exhaustion or the fact that I'd be laid up for days afterwards. The system doesn't take that into account. It still doesn't for that matter.

Two weeks later a letter arrived explaining that I didn't qualify for disability allowance because I could walk with two artificial legs and sticks. Of course I appealed and had to go to the Lawnswood Medical Centre in Leeds for a second interview.

Before I met the doctors I had to go through some preliminaries with a little man in a white coat. My letter spelt it out very clearly that I hadn't to urinate for four hours before the medical so I was bursting when I arrived. First job though was to weigh me.

"Just slip onto the scales please Mr Hirst."

Well I did my best but after five minutes I still had only one foot on. I just couldn't balance. I wish the doctors could have witnessed my efforts because there was no better way to show the problems I faced. The little man in the white coat gave it up as a bad job.

"If you could just provide a sample, we'll dispense with the weighing," he said, as he handed me a sample bottle about the right size for 'Tom Thumb'.

Now I hadn't been to the toilet for four and half-hours and that bottle wasn't as they say in the retail trade, 'fit for purpose'.

I didn't want to leave a puddle on the floor of the cubicle, which was so nicely decorated with a large vase of flowers, or pee in the washbasin, so I decided to improvise.

"Will this do?" I said, handing him a large vase full to the brim.

Finally I met the doctors. Well, met is the wrong word really as they had never spoken to or acknowledged me in any way. They talked to each other and poked and prodded me.

"You can get dressed now lad," was all they said to me. This was the final straw and I lost my temper. I always try to see the funny side of things, you know, take a positive view. I'd accepted the farce of trying to get on the scales and having to take a pee in a vase but this wasn't right.

"I'm nobody's lad," I shouted. "I'm a married man with a family. I'm a human being and should be treated with dignity."

I lost my appeal.

After being turned down twice I was getting desperate until I saw an advertisement in the Daily Mirror for enlisting in the parachute regiment.

I applied and received a letter inviting me for an interview and medical. I thought, 'If they turn me down I will have some evidence to back up my disability claim.' I was serious. I'd have bloody gone to the interview. Mind, knowing my luck I'd have become the first leg-less paratrooper in history.

My final appeal came before I had a chance to serve my Queen and Country.

Two Professors and a Consultant were to examine me. They came into the room where I had been asked to sit. There were three chairs in the room. I was sat in one and my legs were where I'd thrown them, six feet away leaning against another.

They took one look and told me to get dressed.

"You shouldn't have had to come here, Mr Hirst," was all they said.

I got my disability allowance on my third attempt. So there I was at twenty four years of age, a married man with a baby daughter and a severe disability. I was about to start on a new chapter in my life. The cavalier days were over and I felt it was time to give something back.

CHAPTER 6

FAMILY LIFE

Once we had sorted out our financial situation, (we had to sell the little house in Bell Lane and move into a council house), Sheila became our sole wage earner. This was a traumatic time for a man who was used to, and wanted to provide for his family. After one hundred and twenty unsuccessful job applications I reluctantly had to accept work at Remploy as a last resort. (Remploy was an organisation established to help rehabilitate wounded soldiers and when I worked there, many disabled people were employed on very low wages.)

After eighteen months my stumps were ulcerated and the pain stopped me from working altogether. There were no new men in those days.

In Yorkshire at that time, if you did any housework you weren't considered to be 'a man'! Initially, I couldn't accept that I would never work again but after a long discussion with Sheila, we agreed that I would look after the home and she would take a post as a non-teaching assistant. It took me a long time to adjust to the situation. I was no longer the breadwinner and I thought, 'Where does this leave me?'

Like most people at that time, I was conditioned to accept the stereotypical roles of men and women and at first felt my masculinity was under threat. Needs must though and I knew it was right for me to do my share, so that meant becoming a 'house husband'. As always with me, I wasn't going to apologise for my life but rather celebrate it. The Pontefract and Castleford Express published an article about me running our home entitled, *When a Man's Place Is in the Home*. The article explained how much I was enjoying and coping with my role.

"My whites are the whitest in Ackworth," was my boast to the reporter. Boy did I get some stick for that, particularly from the women! Of course it hadn't been easy and when the article was written I still had much to learn. Adventurous cooking for me was any combination of bacon, egg, tomato and beans but, considering that when I started I couldn't even boil an egg, I had come a long way. When the reporter asked me if I didn't feel like experimenting with more exotic dishes, my reply was, "Listen -- when I make bacon and egg it's an experiment. It's never the same twice."

A big positive for me was that Louise my youngest daughter hadn't started school so I was able see her grow and mature and that was an experience I'd missed with my other girls when I was out at work.

I enjoyed my time as a stay at home dad and was never lonely because there were always people calling in for a chat. Eventually, I became pretty efficient, particularly at the cleaning side of things. You know, tidying, hoovering and washing up. Washing the clothes was a different matter. Sheila would leave me piles of clothes with instructions about what settings to use for each load. No automatic washing machines in those days that could think for you; we had a top loading twin tub and you had to know what you were doing. It was a lovely day and there was a pleasant breeze blowing. What we stay at home dads call, 'a good drying day'. I had everything washed and dried quite early in the day and all that was left was the girls' woolly school cardigans. I'd no instructions for washing them but thought, 'how hard can it be? Sheila will be very pleased if I've finished it all before she gets home from work.'

So I put them in the machine on boil wash for half an hour and then rinsed and spun them three times. It was only when I went to peg them out that I realised I was in big trouble!

My girls' beautiful cardigans were unrecognisable. Out of shape, shrunken bits of rags. On the positive side the colours hadn't faded but at that moment I was pulled every which way. Just when I needed to stay calm and collected, I panicked. We had, at that time, a hole in the bottom of our garden that we were slowly filling with garden rubbish. I buried those poor abused garments in this shallow grave and with heavy heart went indoors to put the kettle on. At first, no one noticed that the cardigans had disappeared and I started to breathe a bit more easily.

Over the next week Sheila asked about each cardigan as the girls needed a change of top for school. With a blank face I expressed concern and bewilderment about the whereabouts of the elusive garments and offered the suggestion to a puzzled Sheila.

"Maybe they were left at school." Things quietened down over the next few weeks and I relaxed again. I'd forgotten all about it when, like Scrooge in 'Christmas Carol', my ghosts came back to haunt me.

The following spring, Sheila decided to do a spot of gardening and I was left watching television.

"Look what I've found," she said, as she stood there with Rachel's grubby and mangled cardigan.

"That's a surprise," I said; cool as you like.

"Must have blown off the line."

Sheila disappeared back into the garden but two minutes later had returned with Mel's cardigan and a very suspicious look on her face.

"Look what else I've found," she said.

"Well love it must have been a very windy day," I explained defensively.

When Sheila returned with Ruth's cardigan, I knew the game was up.

"Don't tell me," Sheila smirked, "There was a gale blowing that day."

I never seem to get away with anything.

I certainly never got away with the wardrobe fiasco. A pal of mine built us a new set of wardrobes and they looked really good. He was an excellent carpenter and worked for a funeral director making coffins. What I didn't realise at the time was that the lovely door handles he put on the wardrobes were in fact coffin handles! When we became aware of what had happened we knew straight away we would have to change them. We didn't want people to think we were the 'Addams Family'.

I borrowed a drill and we bought some new brass knobs that Sheila really liked and I set about replacing all the handles. To begin with I worked slowly and meticulously to make sure the handles looked just right. I took ages measuring and marking to ensure the first door would get Sheila's seal of approval, before embarking on the other six. Once I got the go ahead, I thought, 'Right Roy, now you can motor on.'

I completed the job in double quick time, drilling through the doors from the outside with the six inch drill piece I'd borrowed and adding the knobs as I went. When I'd finished, I thought the wardrobes looked first class and shouted for Sheila hoping she would sing my praises for a job well done. She was most impressed until she opened the doors and held up her coat. I now realised that using a six-inch drill to bore through a one-inch door, was not a good idea.

For every hole there was a corresponding ruined garment.

Sheila's jacket had a mangled sleeve and her brand new dress looked as though giant moths had attacked it. If I'd been her, I wouldn't have let me near any more DIY projects but Sheila has such a forgiving nature. The final part of our redecoration of the bedroom was to be a new carpet but there were a number of floorboard nails sticking up. I thought I'd help the carpet fitter by knocking them in and all went well until the last one near the wall by the radiator. When I heard the hissing sound I knew I was in trouble and my DIY days were numbered. On investigation, it became clear that some idiot had put a nail through a hot water pipe and I might have to build an Ark.

I had no idea how to stop the water so I rang a friend of mine, Neil Richmond, who knew all there was to know about plumbing.

"Don't worry, Roy," he said. "Have you a slice of bread?"

"Nay lad," was my reply. "You can eat after you've done the job."

It turned out that he could use the bread to make a temporary seal for the pipe. Marvellous what you learn as you go through life. From then on, when there was serious DIY to be done, I've left it to the experts.

I have a lovely and very supportive family but on occasions, I have had to wonder whether there has been a plot to 'bump me off'. I can't think why because I'm not worth anything but there's definitely a pattern of incidents that make me suspicious.

One day we went to Danes Dyke on the coast. We parked at the top of a steep incline and Ruth began pushing me down the hill. As we gradually picked up speed, I said to her, "Just hold on Ruth, nice and steady." She was obviously not listening since my chair continued to speed up.

"Ruth? Ruth? Ruuuth!" I realised from the heavy silence behind me that Ruth wasn't with me anymore and whatever anxiety I then felt, was doubly reinforced by the astonished looks on the faces of people as I sped past.

I couldn't stop my inevitable progress to the solid face of rock at the bottom of the hill but I made a good attempt. I burnt my hands and scraped my knuckles but slowed myself down to a pace that allowed me to bounce off the wall without breaking my wheelchair or me. Of course, I knew my family were all concerned and would say so in due course, when they'd stopped laughing.

Wells-next-the-Sea, nearly became 'Roy-Wells-in-the Sea'. This time it was Sheila pushing - or not, as it turned out. Same scenario, different location.

Eddy the Eagle on wheels accelerating for take-off. Frantic shouts of, "Grab him!" as my runaway pram came to a screeching halt inches from the edge of the jetty. At least I had the sense to react quickly and brake like mad. There was a horrible smell. I think it was burning rubber but it might have been melting flesh.

Obviously, the women in my family were not up to the task of 'finishing me off', so it was left to one of the men. Again it was holiday time and we were in France. Sheila and I had gone with Mel and her family. We were staying half an hour away from the coast and so we had to take everything with us that we would need for a day on the beach. Having a set of wheels seemed a godsend when we arrived, because everything could be piled on top of me.

Windbreak, towels, games, bags and picnic hamper; the lot all piled on me. I've got long arms but it was still a struggle holding everything and from the front I was almost invisible. Once again we had to negotiate a long steep incline and this time my hands were full.

We set off for the beach with my son-in-law Jack pushing me and I felt reassured that I could rely on Jack's strength and discretion to see me safely down the hill. None of us had taken into account the fine layer of sand covering the concrete incline. Half way down, Jack's feet went from underneath him and my feeling of 'well-being' evaporated. I've always admired

Donald Campbell for breaking all those speed records but now I began to think I might create one myself. Holding on for dear life, I accelerated down that ramp as though jet propelled. I must have been doing about 70 mph or, being in France, the metric equivalent when I hit the sand.

People who know about physics, tell me that if you suddenly stop something moving forward, the energy that has been generated transfers into upward motion. I was about to prove them right. The wheelchair stopped dead but nothing else did. Parasol, picnic hamper and wind-break: everything flew through the air, threatening to decapitate some very surprised sunbathers.

Like a human canon ball, I shot majestically into the air and landed head first in the sand some twenty feet away. It must have been horrendous for innocent bystanders to watch, because the force ripped off my legs and sent them boomeranging in different directions. The sight of me looking like 'Humpty-Dumpty' minus his pants caused quite a commotion but calm was soon restored as everyone could see that I was okay. There was no blood oozing into the sand and as usual everyone in the Hirst family including me, was laughing. The French just wrote us off as another eccentric English family. Can't argue with that really!

To be serious for a moment, I do consider myself fortunate to have such a loving and devoted family. Although my sister June emigrated to Australia in the sixties, my brother Steve and his family still live in Ackworth and all four of my daughters now live in the village. It's great that Sheila and I see them and our grandchildren regularly. I suppose I take it all for granted but need to remind myself of how lonely some people are. We all get along really well but the bonus is that if there is a problem, everyone rallies round.

Rachel, our eldest, is the fiery and independent one and was quite capable at school but like me, she didn't always apply herself. I can honestly say that as a teenager she gave us more trouble than the other three put together. These days she's settled down and doing well, with three children, Laura, Glen and Georgia.

Ruth is the quiet one and at the moment is a full time housewife looking after her two children, Ashley and Arran.

Mel is the organiser. When she's in charge, everything has to be done to a timetable. She's married to Jack and they have three children, Callum, Rogan and Connie. She even finds time to work as a part time receptionist. Finally, Lou, the baby of the family, is the most easy- going of my girls and is married to Michael.

They have two children, Eden and Ellis and Lou is a child minder.

(Left to right) Roy with Lou, Ruth, Mel and Rachel

Roy, Sheila & the family as they are today.

My mother Gladys died in 2004, but for nearly fifty years lived in Chapel Garth, only a few doors away from Sheila and me. She was a regular and very welcome visitor and we all miss her. When she was seventy-nine, she moved into a bungalow because years and years of heavy smoking had ruined her lungs and she couldn't climb stairs any more. She still got around pretty well and visited us all the time, until she was eighty-two and diagnosed with lung cancer.

For the last few months of her life she was house bound and I found that very hard. Her bungalow had no disabled access or toilet and for me she might as well have been on the other side of the world. I did try to visit her but the front door was very narrow and her hallway tiny. I would bump my way through the door and then find I couldn't swing right into the living room. There were only centimetres to spare. Bouncing my chair around a millimetre at a time, I would get into a right lather and scrape the paint off the walls.

It was embarrassing to cause so much damage and when I did finally manage to get in, I just had time for a quick word before turning around to go home to the toilet. This was one of the few times in my life when I really regretted not being able to walk. Not so much for myself, but for my mother. You'd think that in the twenty-first century we'd be beyond such inconveniences.

Although I couldn't visit my mum and felt angry and frustrated about it, I knew my girls were taking good care of her. As their grandmother deteriorated, they organised a twenty-four hour rota and took turns staying overnight. Sheila did her bit when she was off duty and I knew my mother was being well looked after. I felt blessed to have such a close and supportive family but those last few precious months of my mother's life were agony for me to endure.

Roy with Mum and Dad and Dave Waterson

CHAPTER 7

MINERS' STRIKE

I remember very clearly the day I became involved in the miners' strike. I had to be at the Bell Lane polling station by 7.30am because I was the agent for Henry Daley during the local election and there was much to do. By 9.30am I was standing outside the polling station when I was approached by a group of miners who lived in Ackworth.

"Why has Ackworth no miners' support group?" They wanted to know.

"Nobody has asked us," was my weak reply. I knew then that something had to be done.

"Leave it to me, I'll see what I can do," I said.

I talked to a few people and it was decided there and then that we needed a room of our own. There were very few venues in the village but there was a Mission Hall, which was rarely used except for the odd bring and buy or jumble sale.

So I rang the local vicar and he said, "Yes, you can have it. There's no problem at all. Come and collect the keys and keep them as long as you need to."

A few days later I called a meeting and there was a great response, particularly from women.

We organised a committee for the Ackworth Miners' Support Group and I was asked to be Chairman. Now the hard work had to begin and this was new to all of us. We had to go one step at a time. The first question was "What do we need?" We had a kitchen and hot water from a gas boiler but there was no cooker. So once again I was on the phone scrounging for help. The response was tremendous. Within a few hours we had a cooker, fridge, pans, cutlery and cooking utensils. You name it, we had it.

We still were not quite sure what we were going to do, where the money was coming from. This was a very new venture for most of us. I started ringing around, getting advice from charitable organisations and unions. The unions said it was difficult for them to help because they'd already twinned themselves with other support groups. We seemed to have missed the boat because we were a month behind everyone else. We got an offer of fifty pounds a week, which was a beginning and to be honest, at the time we thought was fantastic and accepted gratefully.

The first day we opened we intended to provide a cup of tea and a biscuit but more importantly, a chance for people to meet. We hoped we could become a focal point for the community and over time provide practical support and advice. We were busy that first day. The boiler was never off. Over two hundred people turned up and they all wanted to talk.

Most families were experiencing problems. Debts were building up and rent and mortgages were overdue. People were being threatened with having their gas and electricity cut off.

There was a desperation about folk that I'd never seen before and, as we all know, things were going to get a lot worse before they improved.

I got in touch with the people from the Citizens Advice Bureau to ask if it could provide an adviser. They were great. They sent a chap who was really helpful and from then on he came every day we were open. We were there to try to sort out people's problems not just provide food and drink, although that was important to people who weren't getting enough to eat.

We had to start fundraising to find money for food and in addition to raffles and other local initiatives, I found myself travelling around the area. I went all over talking to groups of people in an attempt to increase donations and educate people about the plight of the miners and their families.

I remember going to Leeds University to talk to the students. I'd never been in a place like that before and it took all my courage to do it. I didn't sleep the night before because I was in a blind panic. I thought, 'How can I talk to these educated people?' When I arrived I was shown into the students' union bar and had to answer questions from about fifty students. I answered all the questions as honestly as I could and after an hour I felt quite confident.

Just when I thought it was all over they took me into a massive room that they used for lectures and it was crammed with people. Suddenly I was looking up at hundreds of expectant faces. I nearly died. I never imagined in my wildest dreams having to address an audience like this. As before, I tried to give a true picture of what I'd experienced and seen. I couldn't believe how they cheered and clapped at the end.

It had been a nerve-wracking experience and I found myself with a lump in my throat, but we collected £500 which was brilliant.

My next job was to drive to Hull and talk to the Dockers. All the things I'd heard about Dockers, you know, the tales of rough, hard drinking, fighting men, but they were absolutely brilliant. I'd gone in my jacket and tie and felt out of place in this rough working environment. These were no-nonsense men and I was their guest. I had dinner in this big primitive hut with some of the union men. When I say dinner, it was mince and gravy on a tin plate with a noggin of bread. It was like a scene out of Dickens.

Everything in that hut was rough but I'll never forget how kind and supportive they were. They took us to a warehouse and told us to take as much food as we could get in the car and on top, they gave me a cheque for £1,000 and asked me to go back every fortnight from then on.

During this time I felt I needed to know more about what was happening to the miners and the local N.U.M.

The office at South Kirkby Pit sent some of us in a van to different picket lines so we could see for ourselves what was happening. I remember the very first time I travelled with a group of pickets.

It was 2.30 am. Not my best time of day usually but on this occasion I was feeling euphoric. By the time the van stopped I was absolutely flying. It didn't dawn on me why I felt high because I've never taken drugs but that day I'd inhaled lots of smoke from all those people who had lit up. I thought everyone was smoking tobacco but obviously not!

My first picket was uneventful but nevertheless was burnt into my memory. I've never been over supportive of the police but I had always respected them and the job they did. At the beginning the police were okay and the jostling between pickets and police was good-natured but that didn't last long. Things changed when they brought in the MET police. Those guys were something else. They deliberately provoked and taunted the miners. I wouldn't have believed it if I hadn't heard it for myself.

They would throw pennies on the floor and shout, "Here, buy your kids a Christmas present."

Some would shout, "My mates having your wife while you're here." Or, "Keep the strike up men, I'm earning a fortune in overtime."

It was designed to provoke confrontation and of course angry men end up doing desperate things.

I remember on one occasion getting to a pit at 5.00 am and having one of the most frightening experiences of my life.

The mounted police were gathered at the top of the hill and we were hemmed in on one side of the road by a line of terraced houses snaking up the hill to the pit and a high wall on the other side. As we were getting out of the van I heard someone shout, "Get out of here."

The horses were coming down the hill and I heard whooshing noises overhead as bottles, some full of petrol, started landing on the road and bursting into flames. One hit our van and set the roof on fire. It was like being in a war zone. I don't condone the times when miners went beyond the law but it was usually as a response to severe provocation from the police. I've also seen when police were standing face to face with miners and then all of a sudden they'd part and let pickets run into the road before closing ranks and trapping groups of miners.

The mounted police would then ride them down and club them. I saw it at Yorkshire Main, Doncaster, Frickley, and South Kirkby. I remember on one occasion I was invited to Knaresborough to speak and before I went I'd already had two letters, threatening that if I went I'd be strung up. Bob Cryer the M.P. and I were the main speakers. I went to the Town Hall and it was absolutely packed. There didn't seem to be a lot of labour supporters. They were asking us some difficult questions and when we answered as honestly as we could, they called us liars.

Limited as I was in public speaking, I could only talk about what the strike meant from a family and community point of view; that a pit closing meant whole communities dying.

"If they close the pit, the shops follow because there's no money for barbers, florists or laundries. It's the domino effect, the knock-on effect."

I passionately believed that the government had provoked this situation and it wanted to close pits as a revenge for what the miners had done to Ted Heath. I didn't go into the politics of it but talked about how people were having their gas and electricity switched off and telephones disconnected. Children had to go cap in hand for free school meals. A lot of schools were brilliant and did what they could for the children but many proud people were crushed.

This meeting was scheduled for an hour but lasted two and a half. After it was over a very elderly vicar approached us. He had a posh accent and said, "I say there."

I thought I'd let Bob Cryer handle him because I felt Bob was a bit more refined than me. He tapped me on the shoulder and more or less accused me of telling lies about what I'd described, particularly my experience on the picket line. What I said to him was what I said to everyone who doubted me.

"Don't take my word for it. Come and see for yourself."

"And how would one go about doing that?" was the reply.

"You would ring me up and say you would like to go on a picket and I would arrange it for you with the N.U.M." I said.

"May I have your telephone number?" He asked.

"You certainly can." I replied.

I thought, 'That's it, I'll never hear from him again.' But about three days later he rang to ask if he could bring three or four different people.

I think he thought it would be like a sightseeing expedition. I tried to explain to him how rough it would be with the pushing and shoving.

Following his call I made arrangements to meet him and the others at Featherstone and then took them to South Kirkby pit and put them in a van which then took us all to Great Houghton. I explained to him that when we got out of the van he was to stay close to me. I explained that the police stood shoulder to shoulder until the mounted police were coming and then they would create a gap for the miners to run into the road to stop the horses and vans coming up.

Sure enough, we were leant against this wall with not much to talk about when the police line opened up and the vicar and another observer followed the miners onto the road to see what was happening. Of course the line closed up and they were trapped on the road. I could hear them saying to this policeman, "Hey, could you let us through? We're observers."

I won't describe what the bobby said but he certainly wasn't going to let them through. These horses came down and every other word was an 'F' word from the mounted policeman.

The vicar tried to intervene and asked the policeman to moderate his speech. As soon as he had spoken the policeman hit him on the head with his baton and he dropped to the ground, poleaxed. The miners dragged him unconscious back through the police line, where I found him with a deep gash on his forehead and a black eye.

Every year since then I've had a Christmas card from him and when he went back home, he sent £3 every week for a sack of potatoes to help the miners and their families. He never doubted after that what I said was true.

Most people saw miners as rough, hard-nosed men. We went to Selby and there were so many cars we blocked the bridge completely and traffic was at a standstill. The van I was in couldn't move and as we were near a farm the lads thought they'd help themselves to some apples to take back for their families and the support group. Some brought a few apples back but within five minutes the others returned with a pig. Well I just couldn't believe that they'd pinched a pig and it was in the back of our van, so I said, "What are you going to do with it?"

"Well, we'll kill it and make some bacon. It'll make some good meals for the next few weeks."

A lot of blank faces met my question and then we had a great debate about where they would kill the pig, who would do it and how it could be cured afterwards. It ended up with one strapping miner who had a reputation for being a hard man, being elected to kill the pig with a hammer.

He went outside with the pig in one hand and the hammer in the other but he just couldn't bring himself to do it. They 'hummed and ahhed' for a good twenty minutes. The traffic still wasn't moving so in the end these rough and tough miners decided the only thing to do was put the pig back.

There wasn't much light relief during this period but on one occasion a group of miners gained a little satisfaction from one prank. After it had snowed some of the pickets built snowmen to look like policemen and this didn't go down well with the boys in blue. No sooner were they built than they were flattened by the police land rovers. This became a bit of a game until one snowman was built over a concrete bollard. The police got quite a shock when they tried to knock that one down because the snowman came off better than the land rover.

One of the other things I'll never forget was the amount of suffering and hurt. Street after street of people with nowhere to turn for help. Some people had families not involved in mining but others had three generations of miners so that everyone was trying to survive on nothing. I'm not just talking about rent, mortgages and heating. Six months into the strike kids were suffering too.

They were short of clothes and shoes and were missing out on a normal social life. No one had money for anything. I could only see the suffering from the outside but I felt for those people. Pressure on families was enormous and some marriages were breaking down.

I got involved with another group that travelled to Nottingham and brought miners and their families into Yorkshire for a bit of respite, since in Nottinghamshire there were very few N.U.M. members on strike because most miners had joined the breakaway union. It was awful because the strikers were being ostracised in their own communities and their children were being picked on and bullied.

I wrote to various Members of Parliament and some sent money. Dennis Skinner was very good. The only person who didn't send a donation was our own MP and that's very sad because he was such a gentleman. I don't think he understood the rules of play because he was an N.U.M. sponsored MP. He was a nice man and just forgot how he'd got where he was and who he should be fighting for. When things were going wrong on the picket lines he didn't ring the union to find out its view, he preferred to ring the Chief Constable and get his view instead. The miners never forgot that, as consequently, he was de-selected.

People were suffering and Christmas was coming up so I decided to have a Christmas party for all the kids. More fund raising was needed and we raised enough money to give all the kids a good present and a smashing Christmas party. It might have seemed a small thing but it was something. I remember a bakery near Barnsley offered us the chance to buy bread buns and cakes for next to nothing and they were regarded as real treats. One day I had a phone call asking if we'd like some free bread and of course I said, "Sure."

I gave them my address and thanked them sincerely. Within two hours two vans pulled up outside my house and in no time at all, my front room was literally full from floor to ceiling with bread. We had to set up a network of people with deep freezers so we could store all this bread before it went off.

It took us hours to sort out but it was worth it because we didn't have to buy any bread for a long time. I learnt a very important lesson that day. After that, when anyone else offered food or goods, I always asked, "How much is there?"

I must mention the wives who were part of the miners' support group. These brilliant women made it all happen. Joyce Evans was an engine driver's wife but she came every day for a year and acted as secretary. She cooked, washed and cleaned. She was always there. The others were full of spirit. They were adamant that they weren't going to give in. They were going to support their husbands through thick and thin. They would keep going for as long as it took and now they had a place to meet they could share their problems. They were no longer on their own. If one was suffering, they were all suffering. They gave comfort and gained strength from each other.

These women had come out of their homes and in a very 'soft' way were beginning to learn about politics. A lot of them went on then into the real political world. Other women organised themselves into self-help groups and went on to further education courses.

Although the strike was a terrible time for the region and many families, it did have a liberating side for these women. Some good came out of the suffering, heartaches and problems. A lot of women realised there was more to life than being at home, caring for families and doing domestic chores. There was an opportunity for them to show just how able and talented they were.

This was real equality of opportunity. You've got to imagine that for 12 months each and every day we opened up the Ackworth miners' support group. When the strike was officially over, the group came to an end and that in itself was a difficult time because people had grown used to supporting each other. For me it was socialism at grass roots, working at its best. The day we closed the group was one of the saddest days I can remember. Washing the floor, stacking the tables and cleaning the Parish Hall until it was spotless was our last act and when I locked that door for the last time I felt a deep sadness.

As I looked around I could see that everyone felt the same way as me and the turn of that key marked the end of something very special to all of us. We had worked tirelessly and without relief for a year. We had fought for resources and helped people survive. We had become a tightly knit group. We cared for each other as well as the cause we served. Suddenly everything just stopped.

In years to come, when children have forgotten about the mines, the strike and the old mining community traditions, there will still be a few of us who will remember and talk about the tragedies and triumphs of those times and the community spirit that carried people through. After the strike was over a number of miners proposed that I was made an honorary member of the N.U.M. I received a letter from the union saying they'd had a ballot and I was now an honorary member. I was thrilled to bits that they'd bestowed this honour on me.

I believe there aren't many honorary members and I'm proud to stand alongside people like Dennis Skinner and Tony Benn.

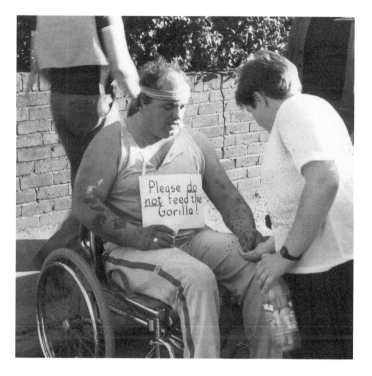

Fundraising for the Miners' Strike

CHAPTER 8

POLITICS

While at Pollard Bearings I joined the union and dealt with quite a few crises, which fired my interest in wider political issues. Tommy Dando, a local councillor, came to see me to ask if I'd stand as a candidate for the Parish Council. I just laughed. I was amazed he'd asked me.

"What, me? Stand for the Parish Council? I know nothing about politics." I said.

"I don't think anyone would vote for me," was my shocked reply.

Tommy didn't give up easily and must have seen qualities in me that I didn't recognise in myself.

"Why don't you come along to a few meetings before you make your mind up," he suggested and that seemed reasonable enough. I'd been a member of the Labour Party since 1963 but was never really active. So I started handing out leaflets and became a general dogsbody. In 1967 I did stand for the Parish Council and was elected. I was a Parish Councillor from then on until I retired. Best time of my life.

I remember my first Parish Council meeting. I was really nervous, wondering what the heck I'd got myself involved with. We met in this old building upstairs and I had to hump myself up the stairs. No chair lift in those days. We sat around these tables and then the public came in. There were a lot of observers and they certainly were not friendly. I couldn't believe how many people were there and how angry everyone seemed to be about all sorts of different things. I thought, 'I don't know what half of them are talking about,' so I kept my mouth shut that night.

After a few months I began to understand that there were quite a number of things that weren't right. I couldn't understand why the Parish Council weren't taking action. No one seemed interested for the future. There was very little to occupy young people. There was a bit of a youth club but we needed something better. Two ladies ran the youth club on a shoestring, with no help from anyone and they did a fantastic job. In those days I wanted to put the world to rights and do everything.

Brackenhill School became surplus to requirements and the Parish Council was asked if they wanted to take its management on board and to this day, I will never understand why it didn't. The councillors said it was going to be a big burden and a liability but what an asset it would be now. Over time I've learned, 'you win some - you lose some'.

The Parish Council wouldn't buy the chapel on Wakefield Road and it's now a lawnmower repair place!

We ought to have had that because we had 'no end' of football or rugby teams that were doing really well and it would have made a fantastic youth club/changing rooms with all sorts of extra facilities.

The Parish Council wasn't prepared to invest in the future. There was no vision or enterprise. There was loads of cheap land available in those days. If we had bought it then, what could we have achieved by now? So for many years I was the only member of the Labour party on the Parish Council and I felt like a voice in the wilderness.

Senior Citizens' Christmas Party 1998
Roy and Dick Dunn with Mayor and Mayoress

Parish Councillor Hirst helping children
from Bell Lane School plan disability access to
Ackworth School.

1981
Wakefield Council's newly formed Cabinet.
(Left to right) Councillors Bob Mitchell, Denise
Jeffery, Betty Rhodes, Peter Box, Frank Ward,
Roy Hirst and Brian Hazell.
(Missing from the picture were Councillors Tony
Dean and Phil Dobson.)

Meeting Nelson Mandela

Roy with Jon Trickett and Frank Dobson

Roy with Gordon Brown

The Political Rounds

Roy with Tony Blair

Roy at Ed and Yvette's wedding

Despite all the frustrations, I was a Parish Councillor for 46 years and am pleased that since 2010, Labour has been the majority party.

On numerous occasions I was asked to become a Wakefield Metropolitan District Councillor. Until the strike I had always turned down the idea because I didn't think I was that good or educated enough. The turning point for me was the miners' strike. I was thrown in the deep end. Public speaking, helping people with their problems, dealing with rent and housing issues. I cut my political teeth by fighting for people and causes I believed in. I'd always been able to fight with my fists but now I learnt to fight using my wits and arguments; by persuasion, compromise and listening to opposing views. After the strike I thought that maybe I had the talent and experience to make a difference and to be of service. I felt that there was much to be done and despite some reservations, in 1991 I stood for the District Council to represent the Ackworth, Crofton and Ryhill Ward.

I regained the seat for Labour with a whopping majority. I was a nervous wreck waiting for the votes to be counted, but I needn't have worried because by then, I was well-known in the community and respected for the work I'd done during the strike and I received three times more votes than all the other candidates put together.

It was a brilliant feeling to win and I was both relieved and excited. This was it. As a District Councillor I felt that I could change the world. I expect I was pretty naïve but there's nothing wrong in my opinion about being an idealist.

I was a little nervous when I attended my first council meeting but I did know a lot of councillors and everyone made me very welcome. It soon became apparent, even on day one, that there were different factions and sub-groups. Depending on where you sat and who you were with, you were soon pigeonholed. Fortunately for me, I seemed to be able to work and get on with everyone and within six months I was elected to three committees. That was when my education really began.

I soon found out that nothing was ever straightforward. At the beginning I wondered if I'd made a big mistake becoming a councillor. I saw everything in black and white. If a family needed a gate for its council house to keep a toddler safe then I couldn't see the problem. Get it sorted. Everything seemed to come down to policies. The family in question wasn't allowed a gate because the house wasn't on a bus route. How daft is that. The smallest improvements seemed to take forever and the more experienced members always had good reasons why something shouldn't happen.

Some of my work as a councillor was very rewarding and worthwhile. I was constantly on the phone helping people with everyday problems. I ran regular surgeries and fought for people's rights. On one occasion, I had a homeless family turn up at my door. It was Christmas Eve and bitter weather. This woman had remarried but was still being harassed by her first husband. He'd broken down the door of her house and the landlord gave her notice to quit. She hadn't been able to find alternative accommodation before the landlord sent men round and threw the family's furniture out into the street.

They'd slept in their car the night before and then travelled from the Midlands to friends in my ward, hoping to be put up for a while. Two families in one small house was a non-starter and so they ended up on my doorstep. Sheila made them something to eat and I got on the phone. I pulled out all the stops and cashed in a few favours and managed to get them into a hostel that night. I also got them on the housing list and I believe the family still live in the Wakefield area. So in my ward I did feel I was making a difference. I decided that I'd been elected for four years and I was going to make the most of it. I've never been a quitter so if the policies weren't working for ordinary people, I was determined to change them.

In twelve months I had established myself and began to make an impact. Most chairs of committees were experienced councillors so I was surprised when I was asked to stand as chair of Equal Opportunities and delighted when I was elected unanimously. This was a job I could really get my teeth into and because of my disability, felt particularly qualified to do.

I couldn't wait to get started and I didn't have to because there was a meeting already arranged for seven o'clock that night with the ethnic minority groups. I was well briefed by the officers about the format and procedures of the meeting and we started promptly at 7 pm. I welcomed everyone and being a little nervous, explained it was my first meeting and apologised in advance for any mistakes I might make. Soon everyone had introduced him/herself and who they represented and I was feeling quite relaxed. The debate was about the best way to create a community centre on the Agbrigg Road.

I listened carefully to everything that was being said and asked my officers to investigate suitable premises. The meeting was buzzing until the clock struck eight.

"Mr. Chairman we are now going to pray."

At that time I knew little about other people's cultures or religions and wasn't quite sure what was happening when everyone began to leave the room.

Thoughts flashed through my mind – 'Was it something I've said? Do they want me to go with them to pray? Is this the end of my political career?'

"Mr. Chairman, we will be back at midnight."

'Bloody hell', I thought. 'I'm not sitting here on my own for four hours.'

As usual, the officers saved the day. They quickly explained the situation to me and we adjourned the meeting, with the promise to reschedule at a later date.

Over the next three years, I made a lot of friends in the Afro-Caribbean and Asian communities and was honoured when asked to open the first ever Mela in Wakefield. I suppose it could be compared to a gala or festival and it was certainly a big success, bringing lots of different groups together. Also in those three years, I got to know my officers very well and developed a strong relationship with them.

On one occasion we had an anti-apartheid meeting in London and had to leave at five o'clock in the morning. Most delegates had stayed overnight but I hadn't been able to. We set off in the car from the town hall with Iqbal Bhana my officer, sitting in the backseat and me next to the driver in the front. I preferred the front because I always had more room. We had a new driver that day, one of the very willing lads they drafted in when necessary.

It was a cold morning and the heater was on full blast. After about half an hour, we all fell silent and I sat watching the traffic as we sped along the outside lane. All of a sudden I thought, 'Blimey, we're getting a bit close here.' I looked at the driver and his eyes were completely shut. I shouted and grabbed the steering wheel. By this time, we were only inches away from the big articulated lorry ahead of us.

As soon as I grabbed the wheel, as a reflex, our driver grabbed me. We struggled for a second or two, no more than that and I had to elbow him to get him to release me to steer the car until he gained control again. We went about half a mile until we pulled up and Iqbal took over the driving. It turned out that the driver had been up since 3 a.m. cleaning and preparing the car. It could have been so much worse. If I hadn't been alert, we would have hit the lorry. Iqbal always tells everyone that I saved his life that day and I know from then on we were like 'blood brothers'.

As Chair of Equal Opportunities, I concentrated quite a lot of my energy into improving disability access. Progress seemed slow but gradually we reduced danger by improving access to public buildings for people in wheelchairs, or parents with pushchairs, by introducing dropped curbs across the Authority.

At that time I was Chair of Governors at Hemsworth High School, which sat on a multi-levelled site. Together with the Headteacher, Dick Dunn, we created wheelchair access to reception, a chair lift into the main school block and sports centre and when the new science block was built, a lift access to the first floor was installed. That was a massive help to me but also any child with mobility problems too. There were still improvements to be made but I know the school has continued to develop its disability access.

In an attempt to make life easier for disabled people I undertook two other developments. The Local Authority and the West Yorkshire travel service agreed to supply an 'access bus service and driver', free of charge for any wheelchair user who telephoned for a lift. Also, after negotiations with the Ridings Shopping Centre management and Social Services, we agreed a space for an electric wheelchair facility. It took six months to arrange this but I was delighted with the outcome. We employed a disabled person to run the scheme and created disabled parking bays adjacent to the wheelchair store and office. We advertised the new facility in local papers and on local radio and soon had five hundred people signed up. It felt good to be making a difference.

Throughout my time as Chair of Equal Opportunities, I was also involved nationally and internationally with the anti-apartheid movement and I was thrilled to receive an invitation from Glasgow City Council to share a platform with Nelson Mandela.

I couldn't sleep much the night before because I thought, 'Here I am, just a village lad without much education, going to meet Nelson Mandela'.

It was a privilege and an inspiration to hear him speak. I was impressed by his total commitment to a non-violent solution to South Africa's problems. He knew that if South Africa was to survive, it would need the efforts and support of both the black and white population. He had a clear vision and was every bit the international statesman. I learnt a great deal from his attitude and approach.

After the official banquet, members of the national executive of the apartheid committee were to meet Mr. Mandela and although I wasn't sure why, I was conducted to a private room.

When I entered, Nelson Mandela was sitting alone. Taken aback, I was a bit lost for words at meeting this great man whom I admired so much.

I needn't have worried because he put me at ease immediately.

"Come in my friend," he said to me. I had a lump in my throat, which returns even now when I think of that moment. I was mystified why no one else was there but delighted to have a 'one to one' conversation with Mr. Mandela. For fifteen minutes I asked him questions and listened to him talk with great passion and authority about South Africa.

He made it quite clear that the most important issue at that time was the economy. He said how vital it was that people like myself, who supported anti-apartheid sanctions, now spoke in favour of new trading links. We had to take action to break down barriers and encourage business, trade and investment in South Africa. He estimated, that with international support, it would still take at least fifteen years for these developments to have a great deal of impact in his country. We had talked about his coming to Britain to make new friends and so he finished our meeting by telling me a story about two friends. The story went as follows. 'One friend would visit the other. He would walk for half an hour before knocking on the door, sitting in a chair by the fire and then filling his pipe with tobacco. Both men would sit smoking, neither speaking to the other. After another half an hour the visitor would get up and, without saying a word, would empty his pipe and leave'.

At this point I was waiting for some sort of explanation, but he didn't offer one. Well I didn't want to ask what the story meant because I didn't want to look really dense. In the end I had to say, "I'm sorry but could you just explain that?"

He just laughed and said, "Friends, true friends don't have to live with each other, don't have to speak to each other, they are just there for each other."

When we parted, he offered me an open invitation to visit him in South Africa and I was left feeling flattered and honoured. It was an unbelievable feeling. I suppose people say things like that and he would be astounded to find me on his doorstep, but it was a wonderfully warm and sincere gesture.

However, not all my trips were as successful as the one to Glasgow.

On one occasion, I was invited to an international conference in Barcelona by a professional organisation who dealt with issues of third world poverty, human rights and equal opportunities and I was keen to attend. After contacting the relevant people in Barcelona and assured that everything would be accessible for someone in a wheelchair, my officer Iqbal Bhana, Councillor Albert Manifield and myself were booked to go and I was looking forward to a lively series of debates.

My enthusiasm was a bit dented when they had to load me onto the tail end of the plane using a forklift truck and I think Albert was having second thoughts as he waited, terrified, for his first ever flight.

I had been assured that the taxi would be a big Mercedes, capable of taking my wheelchair, but at the Barcelona airport there wasn't one to be seen. The first nine taxi drivers in the rank waved me away but finally I found a Good Samaritan.

We had to dismantle my chair and then rope it onto the top of the car, but thankfully, we did all arrive at the hotel in one piece. Not a good start but I thought from now on, things can only get better. So much for my opinion. Things got worse!

The lift in the foyer gave me easy access to my room but first I had to negotiate the flight of steps that led to the hotel entrance. Four hotel staff were hurriedly drafted in to lift me up the steps. I felt quite sorry for them because I'm heavy and bulky and they looked as thin as chips.

With a considerable effort they managed to hump me up the steps and into the hotel. The lift was just a touch too small and so once again I had to dismantle part of my wheelchair to squeeze in. It was with considerable relief that I finally reached my room.

The following day I discovered that the restaurant was down two flights of stairs and so for the rest of my stay I ate on my own at a special table they provided for me in the foyer. I observed all the guests coming and going and they watched me eating my poached egg on toast while trying to look inconspicuous.

The conference centre was across the square and, once more having been carried down the hotel steps like the Queen of Sheba, I was pleased to see a lift at ground floor level. The lift whizzed me up to the conference floor and the doors opened to reveal a massive, U.N.-style room.

This was equipped with personal desks and headphones through which interpreters would offer translations for the delegates. Most impressive! My immediate problem though, was to get past the large concrete pillar stuck right in front of the lift! With a bit of pushing and shoving I managed to scrape into the room but was left wondering what idiot designed that particular feature.

Obviously, the architect was able-bodied and was also responsible for designing the toilets which were up a flight of stairs. That bit of information only became apparent at coffee time! I had the choice of finding an alleyway and peeing behind a car or going back to my hotel.

As the official representative for Wakefield Metropolitan District Council I felt honour bound to do the right thing and chose the hotel. So my 'lifters' had to be summoned and these now dispirited helpers got me in, then later, out of the hotel. In all I was away from the conference for an hour. After attending the evening banquet provided by our host, which required me being lifted up another flight of stairs to the banqueting hall, I decided I'd had enough. I was going home! However, I hadn't reckoned on non-transferable tickets and so found myself stranded in Barcelona for four days.

I learnt a lot about disability on that trip, particularly when it came to people's attitudes. Every time I left the hotel, people would cross themselves. Apparently, most disabled people there didn't leave their homes very often and I was told that many people thought that disability was a punishment for some sin committed in a previous life. It all seemed a bit medieval to me but if it was true, I must have been up to no good in former times. Well I had four days to occupy myself in Barcelona and there was no way I was staying indoors. There were no dropped curbs on the raised causeway so I stuck to the road and left the cars and taxis to swerve around me, pipping their horns in frustration.

It seemed to me that being disabled wasn't a punishment but being disabled in Barcelona could be if I let it. Albert kept me company for the rest of what proved to be, a very interesting week. Sitting by the marina, we watched a crocodile line of children walking with their teacher who were particularly interested in my wheelchair and me and kept glancing in my direction.

For a bit of fun, I took my empty trouser leg and put it round my neck like a scarf, with my foot resting on my shoulder. One child spoke to the teacher about what he had seen. I was hoping that they might come over and speak to me, but the teacher smacked the child hard across the face and they all walked on. It was meant to be a bit of daftness but Albert and I were both shocked by the outcome. Later in the day, we were sitting outside the hotel enjoying the sun when we attracted the attention of a young woman. She kept talking to us in Spanish so we had no idea what she wanted. It finally dawned on us that she was a 'lady of the night' determined to ply her trade. I thought, 'There's only one way to get rid of her.'

"Hold my hand." I said to Albert.

"What?"

"Hold my hand, if she thinks we're gay, she'll leave us alone."

Albert nearly jumped out of his skin. I've never seen a man so affronted!

"Bugger off," was his curt reply.

On our last day, we decided to have a relaxing time in the mountains. A bit of sightseeing. With Albert pushing, we eventually reached a pleasant olive grove where the mountainside levelled off. To our surprise it was full of men. I think there were about thirty altogether. I've always been one for making new friends and headed over towards them hoping for a chat. No one seemed pleased to see us and one man, spotting Albert's camera, pointed at it before drawing his index finger across his throat.

I suppose the black berets and shirts were a bit of a giveaway. We had stumbled across a group of Basque Separatists who were not happy at the intrusion. We were off like a shot and got a pretty frosty reception from the police when we arrived back at the bottom of the mountain. I think the conference delegates would have learnt a lot more following me around all week than sitting in that conference.

When I was asked to become 'Chief Whip' for Wakefield Council, I was happy to take on the role but didn't really understand what it entailed. I wrote to central office and various other authorities to try to define my role and it came as quite a shock when I discovered the extent of the power of my office.

The Chief Whip was responsible for deciding who would serve on which committees but also for discipline. It was my job to make sure that people turned up to committees and voted. This included the Leader of the Authority. As you can imagine that took a lot of my time.

Some days I was in my office at 7.30 a.m. not leaving until 8.00 p.m. but I was determined to do a good job. Not much got past me and with the aid of Susan and then Margaret my secretaries, who gave me immense support, I was allowed to focus on what really mattered.

The three years I was Chief Whip proved to be a very trying time.

Allegations were rife about corruption in councils and in Doncaster, councillors were being prosecuted. I knew politicians in and outside of the council who were unhappy about what was happening in Wakefield and some were talking to anyone who would listen.

I felt it was just a matter of time before the police would be involved, so I wasn't surprised when Colin Croxall, the leader of the Council, called several of us into his office.

He told us that the police were coming into County Hall to investigate the running of the Wakefield Council. Colin explained he was stepping down until after the investigation.

He wanted to free himself up to give the police full support and cooperation on what he thought, would be a wide scale enquiry.

Norman Kennedy, his deputy, was to take over his role, since it was to be business as usual. This was a very traumatic time for all of us and very quickly, Norman found the situation intolerable and decided to resign and concentrate on his family and normal councillor duties.

I suppose I was left 'holding the baby' at least in the short term. The first day the police arrived we were all asked to leave our offices and wait in a meeting room. They confiscated all our computers and although mine was returned pretty quickly, others were not so lucky. In the end there were no prosecutions. Whether that was because we were all innocent or the police couldn't find enough evidence, none of us knew. I never had anything to hide but, like everyone else, I was just relieved that it was all over.

When the leadership became permanently vacant, I was asked to put myself forward but I declined. I didn't think I had the skills for the job, so instead I supported Peter Box who I knew to be a man of integrity, a forward thinker. I was pleased to see him elected to a new era and it wasn't long before the government decided on the cabinet structure as a way of improving local authority decision-making. I was one of the first cabinet members for Wakefield and the responsibilities seemed enormous.

We were making decisions that affected the future of 250,000 people and investing millions of pounds to improve the economy and infrastructure. Sometimes I had to pinch myself because at heart, I was still the little boy from Ackworth that many people expected to stay at home, nursing his disabilities and vegetating. I wasn't to last long in the new set up.

A new leader brings with him a new style and I found myself at times in conflict with Peter. Not with what we were doing, but some of the time, with how we were doing it. After the traumas of the police investigation it was important that everything was open and transparent and one way to do this was for members of the cabinet to have a much more formal relationship with other councillors.

I never saw the need for that and I continued to have between ten and thirty councillors through my door every day. It was how I worked best but I expect some people might have seen conspiracy in my actions. My health was particularly bad at the time and I decided that I would not stand as a councillor at the next election. It was an ideal time to replace me and I tried to accept the situation with good grace.

The cabinet needed new blood and people with the energy and health I didn't have. Wakefield Council needed internal stability not internal wrangling, so I went without a fuss and I'm delighted to see how well the new cabinet is doing. I had been a District Councillor for 13 years and left with no regrets.

Throughout my political life I have always taken a particular interest in health care issues. When I was still a Parish Councillor, I became involved in the Community Health Council. This is a watchdog body for overseeing health care in the area and eventually I became Chairman of the organisation. We dealt with patients' complaints and were supposed to be a key consultative body for hospitals planning their changes. In addition, whenever possible, we would try to provide positive PR for the local NHS services.

We also organised protest marches and petitions on behalf of hospitals under threat of closure and headed delegations to Conservative ministers in a futile attempt to keep local hospitals open. Under the Conservative Government I saw Ward Aldam, Southmoor, Ackton and Castleford hospitals close. In a private capacity, I'm now fighting to save Pontefract General Infirmary. I don't want to see people having to travel to the far side of Wakefield or Dewsbury for their medical care. This was the hospital that saved my life and it's still desperately needed.

I resigned from the Community Health Council in order to become a director of the Primary Care Trust. The Labour Government established PCTs and they had two important functions: to help with policies for local GP practices, but also to act as brokers between those practices and hospitals. They are non-political and to become a director I had to apply and be interviewed by the Secretary for Health.

The directorship was supposed to involve one day a month but with all the problems, workload for non-executives was enormous. Our PCT worked with twenty-six different GP practices and had a budget of one hundred and fifty million. We were responsible for buying hospital beds and services on behalf of GP practices and that was a massive responsibility.

My main role was as Chair of Risk Assessment and I was delighted that our PCT gained a 2* rating for its risk assessment, which I'm told was one of the highest in the country.

As PCTs and hospitals seemed to be held jointly responsible for financial matters, we had to return a large pot of money to the Regional Health Authority to help bail out the over-spend of our local hospitals. Consequently, many of our more exciting plans had to be curtailed.

I expect that I could have turned up for one day a month and taken my money, but that's not my style. I found myself working two, sometimes three days a week and with failing health, felt I'd had enough. With a heavy heart I resigned. Towards the end of my political career there wasn't much about my local area that I didn't know and I had a considerable network of friends, colleagues and supporters. I'm pleased to say that my word was respected and carried considerable weight and anyone needing advice about the political intricacies of our area would come to me.

Colin Burgon rang me one day and asked if he could bring a friend round to talk to me. He was very secretive about who it was, but I said, 'Yes of course they could come.' He arrived with Jon Trickett, the Leader of Leeds City Council. He was a smart, tall man and he wanted to ask me a few questions about the MP vacancy for the Hemsworth Constituency.

Jon and I had a long chat and although it had always been customary for the Labour party to nominate a local candidate, I felt that he had much to offer. Since the miners' strike our area had been abandoned by successive Conservative governments and had been left to decline. Social and economic problems were causing widespread misery and we needed someone to champion our cause. I felt that Jon could be that man and he certainly seemed to have the right credentials. He had brought business and new developments to Leeds, which was now a booming city

I asked Jon why he wanted to be an MP, given the power and success he had in Leeds. He told me he felt he had more to give on a national level and could bring massive experience and skills to the regeneration of the Hemsworth Constituency. Not having a local man would be a big change for us so I wasn't certain about supporting Jon at first, but after many meetings and discussions, I decided he was the best man for the job. I gave him my blessing and support and was pleased when he was nominated as Labour party candidate for the ensuing by-election.

Once Jon was nominated, I became what might be described as his sub-agent. We discussed every issue at length and became very close, almost like brothers. Jon was invited to meet the shadow cabinet and had it cleared for me to go with him to Parliament. Imagine stepping into that arena. We arrived for the meeting and were waiting in the Chief Whip's Office. It was at this point that I made my Parliamentary mark, in more ways than one! To get to the meeting room, I had to pass through a very narrow doorway and managed to get my wheelchair stuck solid. The ushers arrived in their black suits and 'dickey bows' but they were unable to move me. Then two sergeants at arms came and all four of them were pushing and shoving.

They got me out eventually but not before they had taken great chunks out of the doorframe.

Jon tells me that my marks are still there today. Eventually, after about half an hour, we entered the shadow cabinet office where all the famous people who I'd only ever seen on television were gathered.

Jon introduced me and I sat listening to the discussion. Then they asked me if there was anything I wanted to say.

'Well, I thought, here I am. My first speech to the Shadow Cabinet.'

I explained that although the area had always been staunchly Labour, there had been a split between the N.U.M. and the party and Arthur Scargill would have someone standing in opposition to Jon. To guarantee success, it was important that the Labour hierarchy visited the constituency to support Jon's campaign.

They agreed they would come and without exception that promise was kept. It was an amazing feeling to see all these 'big hitters' walking the streets, talking to people. They visited schools and hospitals and generally showed an interest in our area. This left not only members of the party, but also many voters, with a feeling that life was going to get better. There was an optimism and buzz about the place that I'd not felt for a long time.

Needless to say, Jon was elected with a massive majority and Labour won the next general election with a landslide victory.

I met Yvette Cooper at a seminar in Leeds when she was a reporter for one of the big daily papers. She told me she had been to the USA to campaign for Clinton in the presidential elections. I asked if she was interested in becoming a politician and wasn't surprised when a few months later she rang me for advice. I was able to give her some useful contacts and of course, since then she was elected to the Pontefract seat and has become a junior minister. We became good friends and she and her fiancé Ed Balls were regular visitors to my home.

Quite a few local politicians, including myself, were very impressed with Ed and urged him to stand for parliament in the Wakefield area. When he finally agreed, my first response was, "Can you afford the drop in salary?"

Yvette and Ed are very talented people but also very genuine. They relate well to everyone and as a result, are popular and trusted. I'm sure we'll see a lot more of them both in the future.

Before I joined the Labour party in 1963, I had read books by a number of traditional socialists like Keir Hardie and for me politics seemed very simple.

As a socialist I believed in equality for everyone, no matter what colour, creed or religion.

It was all about caring and sharing. Here we are in 2006 and I'm no longer sure what socialism is about or where New Labour is taking us.

I passionately believe that what goes around comes around and that my brand of socialism will come again, socialism based on a shared and devolved power within communities and not centralised control: the men in suits.

I've supported New Labour because it seemed to be the only way to gain power and redress some of the worst inequalities in our society. My party contains good and bad politicians, idealists, pragmatists and opportunists as does all the other parties.

We can all be proud that we have done many positive things to reshape our society but we have also undertaken changes that I find hard to accept and it sits uncomfortably with my brand of socialism.

I believe we have missed a golden opportunity to help those most vulnerable in our communities. I thought we would do much more for the disabled, the elderly, and the weakest members of our society. We've paid lip service to that but we haven't done it.

I believe the situation has deteriorated and the disabled and elderly are worse off than under the Tories.

There will be clever and highly qualified Labour politicians who will tell me I'm wrong; that I don't understand the economic constraints and the political sensitivities. However, after all these years I still see things with a simple clarity. If we really wanted to do it, we could.

CHAPTER 9

LIVING WITH DISABILITY

After I lost my second leg, I offered to go into primary schools and talk about my life and disability. I must have visited about thirty schools in all and had quite a routine going by the end. The children seemed very interested as I talked and answered questions. I was very strong and agile in those days and could perform handstands and other little tricks to demonstrate how physically capable I was despite having no legs.

I received lots of 'thank you' letters from children and my favourite, which I still have, was the little boy who wrote, 'Dear Mr Hirst, thank you for the talk you gave us. When I grow up I want to be a clown just like you.'

I never thought of myself as disabled. Nor did I ever feel disadvantaged until other people built barriers in my way. I'd lived with one leg for many years and nothing had stopped me doing everything I wanted. It came as a shock when in my twenties I faced the possibility of being permanently in a wheelchair.

As a father with a young baby and a wife to support, I suddenly found myself facing the loss of both legs.

Regardless of physical problems, the mental anxiety was worse. Accepting the limitations on my life and worrying about how I would cope with this new challenge was very difficult. Sheila, as always, never doubted me and that inspired me to make the most of the opportunities life presented but no one must ever doubt the anguish I went through at that time.

No matter how long I have lived with my disability, I still experience 'mad moments' that are hard to explain. I have been known, after a few drinks, to jump out of bed in the middle of the night to go to the lavatory. I wasn't drunk but maybe half asleep and I've landed flat on my face on the floor. It was hard to understand why I'd done it, except there must be a part of me that still doesn't accept my legs have gone.

The feelings are always there, the itching and cramps. The nerve attacks are the worst. It feels as though my legs are there and my muscles are in spasm.

The pain can be over quickly or can last for days. I usually wait for about an hour to see if the cramps are going to subside and then I reach for the painkillers.

On numerous occasions, my disability has been inconvenient and the source of many hours of reflection. In other words, I've spent a lot of time hanging around. Sometimes it's been my own fault, other times circumstances have contrived against me. In the days before mobile phones, it has been known for me to be stuck in my own garage for hours on end.

For example, when my stumps were giving me problems, the medical staff at Chapel Allerton would put me in my car without attaching my legs. This was all right as far as I was concerned because my car was hand operated.

They would place my new legs in the boot of the car and off I would go, confident that as usual there would be someone at home to help me. I'm a slow learner because on at least three occasions, I was stranded in my car in my garage until Sheila came home from work. Having finally learnt my lesson, I was very upset the day I arrived home to find the Gas Board had dug up my path. Despite the fact I had left my wheelchair strategically placed ready for me to get out of my car, there was a 3ft. trench between freedom and me. More thinking time!

On one occasion, I had to attend a meeting at the Bradford Town Hall with Councillor David Lunn. Neither of us had been to this town hall before and had trouble locating the lift, which wasn't in the foyer.

It was one of those old fashioned types with manual sliding doors. There was just enough room for me in my chair so David pushed me in, pressed the button for the third floor and pulled the doors closed. I reached the third floor well before David and only then did I realise my predicament. I was like an astronaut strapped in for take-off, except I had no control over the spaceship! I couldn't manoeuvre my chair and I had my back to the control panel. I couldn't get to the lift doors and I couldn't even see if there was anyone waiting for the lift.

Before my companion could arrive, someone else had summoned the lift and off I went again. Every time the lift was coming to a stop I would hear different people call out, "It's okay, I'll take the stairs," and they were off before I could stop them.

After about twenty minutes of 'yo-yoing' up and down, I decided that the next time the lift was coming to a halt, I would start yelling at the top of my voice until I was rescued. As it turned out it was David Lunn who was waiting for the lift.

"Where have you been?" He said.

"Don't ask," was my reply.

People are well intentioned, but I couldn't always guarantee the outcome of their good will. My car was out of action and Colin Burgon (now M.P. for Elmet) offered me a lift to a meeting. We arranged to meet afterwards at the disabled entrance at the side of the building. After the meeting, I forgot about the time as I was talking to Graham Isherwood and one or two other colleagues.

I arrived at the rendezvous point at 9 p.m. and there was no sign of Colin. 'Not to worry,' I thought. 'He's probably talking to someone at the main entrance.'

By 10 p.m. I was getting a bit anxious so I set off around the outside of the building. Not only was Colin not at the main entrance, the whole place was locked up and I was locked out. At 10.30 p.m. I decided Colin must have forgotten about me and it was time for me to get myself home.

As I sat there in my wheelchair a group of young men walked past and I asked them to ring home for me. They'd just left what looked like a derelict house and had clearly been abusing one substance or other because they were too spaced out to understand me.

At 11 o'clock I set off to push myself the twelve miles to Ackworth. Just at that moment I saw a taxi coming and I wheeled myself into the middle of the road. I'd had enough; it was either get a taxi home or die trying. The taxi driver didn't have a fare and I was soon on my way.

Even when everything is officially organised things can go wrong, well for me anyway. At one time I was involved with the Citizen's Band Radio Club and a group of us decided to raise money to buy equipment for a blind lad called Malcolm. We all volunteered to do a marathon, which would end up at the town hall in Wakefield.

We were scheduled to meet the mayor at four o'clock and I was hoping for a brass band and sandwiches. The route would take us from Hemsworth market, through Ackworth, Featherstone, Normanton and finally Wakefield.

I arranged for my friend, Dave Boakes, to help push me and we set off at a cracking pace. Dave was a fit, strong and pretty determined man but by the time we reached Featherstone he was physically exhausted and started vomiting from the exertion of pushing a 'heavy weight' like me.

We were both paying the price for making a spur of the moment decision, leaving no time for training. I soldiered on alone and I can remember getting to the 'Pineapple Pub', where some reporter pushed a microphone in my face and asked me how I felt. I would have throttled him if my hands weren't raw and bleeding and my arms utterly exhausted.

Soon I could see the cathedral spire and with the song 'Chariots of Fire' coursing through my head I renewed my efforts. Needless to say, by the time I reached the town hall it was six o'clock and apart from a few exhausted runners, everyone had left. No Mayor: no Marshals: no sandwiches: no triumphant entry. To make matters worse, those that were there quickly jumped into cars and suddenly I was left, a solitary figure sitting in a wheelchair outside the town hall, bursting for a pee!

That seems to be the story of my life but as is also usual with me someone came to my rescue. A porter from the town hall appeared on one of his security rounds and sorted me out. I arrived home safe and sound with bleeding hands but dry trousers.

I am grateful to the medical profession for all the help I have received but sometimes things have gone wrong in ways that I now regard as funny. I always received a new pair of legs in anticipation of my old ones breaking down. I would take them home in a box and store them until needed. When I eventually started to wear my new legs I had terrible problems walking.

New legs always take a while to master so I wasn't too concerned at first but after a month I knew something was very wrong.

I was walking like a duck because I was lurching to the left every couple of paces and unless I wanted to walk around in circles, I had to over correct to the right every third step. People thought I was Chubby Checker, you know, the guy who invented 'The Twist'. I finally gave up and consulted the doctor who asked me about my shoes and checked me walking up and down his surgery. He quickly got to the bottom of the problem. I'd been given two right legs!

Finding out that I had diabetes was something else to come to terms with but you can always find the funny side of things, sometimes without looking for it. I went to see my GP for a check-up after my diagnosis and was confronted by an earnest young man, determined to be very thorough. He explained that it was very important to keep an eye on my feet, particularly the blood circulation and would I take off my shoes and socks. He obviously hadn't had a chance to look back through my notes and I didn't want to embarrass him so I simply said, "I don't think that will be necessary, doctor."

"I'm the doctor here, I'll decide what's necessary," he insisted. Well I'd done my best, so I thought I'd let him get on with it. When he pulled my sock down his face turned grey. He was so embarrassed and apologetic but as we talked, he also began to see the funny side and we both were smiling when I left.

I seemed to have been the source of embarrassment for a number of medical staff over the years since I don't fit into the usual patient mould.

When I had high blood pressure, I had to have an electro cardiograph at Pontefract General Infirmary. The female technician explained the procedure and started wiring up my chest and arms and then she rolled down my socks. Without saying a word she walked out of the room.

When she returned she was full of apologies and explained to me that seeing my artificial legs had 'just thrown her'. We puzzled for ages about the best way to fit the wires and after consulting her superior officer, we removed my legs and wired up my stumps.

Of course, having no legs has led to unforeseen problems. When I was Chairman of Governors at Hemsworth High School, I arrived for a meeting and parked at the rear of the library, which had a disabled access. It was dark and as I went to put my feet on the ground, I wasn't able to feel that it sloped steeply away from my car. Suddenly my legs slipped from under me and I found myself suspended by my arms. One was trapped in the door-jamb and the other was wedged behind my headrest. I rolled out of the car and only then did the pain hit me. I was lying flat on the floor and I tried to sit up but my arms wouldn't work. When the ambulance arrived, they couldn't lift me because the only way to pick me up was under the arms but both were dislocated. They had to roll me onto a blanket to lift me into the ambulance and use a load machine to lift me into the X-ray room.

My shoulders were dislocated and all the surrounding ligaments torn. It took four doctors to manipulate the joints back into place and it was quite difficult because they couldn't get a good grip on my body and because of the size of my hands and forearms, they were finding it hard to pull my arms. I was losing the circulation in one arm because of a trapped blood vessel so the consultant had to move quickly. I felt like the rope in a tug of war match.

Without any painkillers, they snapped my shoulder back in place and it felt like being hit with a shotgun blast. The doctor suggested I stay in hospital and that they might try traction. I couldn't see how that would be possible since they'd have no legs to grip onto. "It might work if you staple my arse to the ceiling," was my curt reply, as I insisted on being discharged. So I was allowed home and spent the next month in bed with my arms bound to my side.

I couldn't even scratch my nose but was grateful to have a nurse as my wife. The pain lasted for a few months but in more recent years has returned and I can no longer rely on my great shoulder strength to lift myself in and out of the bath or my car. So recently a young occupational therapist visited me to assist with my latest problems.

Roy with David Lund trying out the newly
installed chairlift at Castleford Civic Centre

Roy and Albert in Barcelona

In 1976, Doctor McRoberts sorted out a chair lift for me. I didn't ask for or expect one but nevertheless, it was an added bonus in my life. Eventually it was declared obsolete and dangerous, so I applied for a new one. As Sheila was working and I was a district councillor, our joint income was £3 a week over the entitlement threshold. The chair lift was going to cost us £1,500 which was a lot of money in those days. With bringing up four children, that was money I didn't have. I told the occupational therapist all this and she was amazed I could get upstairs.

"I crawl up on my front and when I get to the bed I have a pile of books which I stack up systematically until I'm sitting on top and Sheila comes and shoves me into bed."

She seemed shocked that I didn't have a chair lift but I said, "I'm not bothered. It's the only exercise I get these days."

I prefer a bath to a shower but it's getting harder for me to manage so the occupational therapist has promised me a special stool for my shower. I refused to have one of those commode type chairs because I feel a man has to have some dignity left. I do take a shower and have sat on the shower floor many times but until now a bath has been easier. Also, given my anatomy, I'm a bit like a sink plunger and I didn't want my arse suctioned to the floor. Have you ever noticed how people in wheelchairs are treated differently from the able bodied? When I lost my second leg, I was determined to walk with sticks and for twenty-five years that's exactly what I did.

I had lots of arguments with doctors who wanted me in a wheelchair for sound medical reasons. I'm a big man and in the Town Hall I had a lot of walking to do from one meeting to another. My short stumps took a hammering and the skin would split and bleed. As a consequence, I was constantly plagued by ulcers.

In 1988 a new firm began supplying my legs and although I knew what I needed, from then on I never seemed to be able to get a comfortable pair. By 1992 I had resigned myself to the fact that I would have to use a wheelchair. It never made any difference to the way people perceived me in political spheres but it did everywhere else.

Once a person is in a wheelchair people seemed to think that he or she is not only physically disabled but also mentally. You become invisible or at least diminished; you are ignored. People asking for the time or directions always ask the person pushing me. Cafes are my favourite places.

"Does he take sugar?" is one of the usual questions.

I soon put them right!

Roy and Roger Brown in the first Ackworth
Half-Marathon.

Roy and Dave Boakes in the marathon.

EPILOGUE

Well I've come full circle. I'm back in Ackworth where I started. No outside commitments. I feel content with my life and what I've achieved.

The social worker came the other day about a stair lift (don't think there's much hope of getting one) and I said to her, "I go to bed on a night and only 50% of me gets into bed. No teeth, no legs, no hair. Poor eyes, Diabetes, High blood pressure, but I still get up smiling in the morning."

Many years ago, I met a young woman called Susan, at Chapel Allerton Hospital in Leeds. We were both waiting for artificial limbs to be fitted. She was only fifteen and had been born without arms or legs after her mother had taken thalidomide during her pregnancy. She was irrepressible. She laughed and joked with me and I could see that absolutely nothing was an obstacle to her.

She's been an inspiration to me and for the past thirty years, whenever I have felt down and sorry for myself I've thought of Susan.

I have this vision of her still smiling and getting on with her life and it helps me understand that there are many people in this world far worse off than me and I have a lot to be thankful for. If I'm remembered at all, I hope people will say, *'he was a caring man.'*

"Does he take sugar in his tea?"

Hello; why not ask me?

I might have a disability,

But to answer for myself I still have the ability.

Just 'cos I'm not stood up like you:

Does not mean there is very little for myself that I can do.

Some people think we're sick

And others a little bit thick.

- Michael W. Williams, Connah's Quay

Roy and Sheila

Roy & Sheila surrounded by their family.

In memory of
Jack Green

BV - #0024 - 161019 - C0 - 198/129/9 - PB - 9781916202399